The
KENSINGTON
CHRONICLES

Charles Lutz

Copyright © 2021 by Charles Lutz

All rights reserved. This book or any portion thereof may not be reproduced or used in any manner whatsoever without the express written permission of the publisher except for the use of brief quotations in a book review.

ISBN: 979-8700257282

The photos in this book were taken by the author, unless otherwise indicated.

Cover design copyright © 2021 by Laurella Lutz

Keywords: Nativism — Immigration — Catholicism — Saint John Neumann — Kensington, Philadelphia — White Flight — Racism

The Happy Self-Publisher
publish, smile, repeat

www.happyselfpublisher.com

For Marina and Ellie

ACKNOWLEDGMENTS

Bringing this book to light was greatly facilitated by virtue of the help received from the following persons: Jeremy Penna, Lois Hoffman, Robin Glanden, Fran Ryan, Brian Daley, S.J., and Laurella Lutz. I am grateful for having had the opportunity to access digital newspaper archives held by the Morris Library of the University of Delaware. I am also indebted to the Library Company of Philadelphia for the several images from their archive that I was able to use. I take full responsibility for whatever errors that remain in the text.

TABLE OF CONTENTS

Acknowledgments 5
Introduction 9

PART I: Upper Kensington 15

A brief geographical orientation 17
"K & A" 21
The Ascension 23
The Street Life of Upper Kensington: a Reminiscence. 45
McPherson Square 51
South of the Square 59

PART II: Lower Kensington 71

Norris Square and Environs 73
"Newt's" and the Kensington Depot 79
Nativism and the 1844 Nativist Riots 83
Aftermath of the Riots: the New Saint Michael's 109

PART III: John Neumann 117

The Neumann Shrine at St. Peter's 119
A Short Biographical Sketch of John Neumann 127

PART IV: A Theological Reflection 147

John Neumann and Sainthood 149

The Parochial School System	163
Epilogue	185
Timeline	193
Works Cited	199
Footnotes	201

INTRODUCTION

I was a formidable walker in my youth. Still am. However, while today the cardiovascular benefit of walking is much heralded, nothing was further from my young mind during my marathon walks. I was rather an unwitting disciple of that great high priest of walking, Henry David Thoreau, for whom walking, which in his case involved ambling through a rustic landscape, bestowed much consolation of soul. Thoreau understood walking to be an art and a holy activity, and expressed a fondness for the word "sauntering," which, he opined in his essay "Walking," likely derives from the expression, "a la Sainte-Terrer." That is to say, pilgrims travelling to the Holy Land in the Middle Ages, when questioned about where they were going as they traversed the countryside, would respond: "a la Sainte-Terrer," that is, "to the Holy Land." Thus was such a pilgrim referred to as a "Sainte-Terrer," or "saunterer." A fanciful derivation? Possibly, as Thoreau himself acknowledged. But his etymological proposal was too irresistible for him.

My early devotion to walking did not, however, conform exactly to Thoreau's vision of an activity uniquely beneficial to the soul. The reason for that has to do with where I grew up and where my ambulatory exertions took place. I happened to be thrown into the world in the middle of the 20th century in the densely-populated and heavily industrialized neighborhood of North Philadelphia known as Kensington. It is unlikely that Thoreau would experience much spiritual sustenance while sauntering along the streets of Kensington. Such walks as I undertook were not exactly nature walks, unless weeds pushing up through cracks in the sidewalks or greenery gone to seed in the occasional vacant lot qualifies for nature. Such bits and pieces of flora give evidence perhaps of the tenacity of nature—a nature not to be denied even in the most urban of environments. For the most part, prevailing in Kensington are asphalt, concrete sidewalks, and the masonry of brick rowhouses, factories, and churches.

Kensington burgeoned as a congested urban enclave and as a beehive of industry in the 1830s and 1840s, earning it the epithet, "workshop of the world." Strictly speaking, though, Kensington was a suburban town at that time, since it was not consolidated into Philadelphia until 1854. The signature brand of industry in Kensington was the manufacture of textiles, and textile mills sprang up like mushrooms during the latter half of the 19th century. Constructed amid these mills were the long stretches of rowhouses that Kensington is noted for, and that furnished laborers with conveniently located but modest residences. The mills seemed to operate around the clock, and many a Kensington resident drifted off to sleep at night, at least before the Post-Industrial era, to the mechanized hum of textile looms. But it must be said that the industrial contour of the environment bore scant resemblance to Blake's "dark, Satanic mills." For the most part, there were no long banks of smokestacks belching out billows of black smoke, no clanging machinery shooting out showers of sparks, nor, at the end of the day, did factories disgorge a procession of dazed workers with sweaty, soot-covered faces. With a few exceptions, the yield of these mills was fabric, not metal.

If the habitats where Thoreau experienced communion with nature were rich in everything the wilderness has to offer, they also tended to be sparsely populated. Thoreau usually went about his nature walks alone, though on occasion with a companion, and his interpersonal encounters along the way were infrequent, though not necessarily inconsequential. He took particular delight in encountering the occasional individual who was as irascible as he was. The solitude experienced in the wilderness was indispensable to the activity's sacred purpose. Kensington, on the other hand, has bustled with people ever since its factories served as magnets for migrants from Europe seeking employment. These 19th century immigrants left their native lands, which, for the most part, were Ireland and Germany, seemingly with few regrets. They were determined to build a new life in the land which represented for them freedom and opportunity. For these largely indigent immigrants, the past was without relevance and was relegated to the black hole of oblivion, or so it seemed. Consequently, the descendants of these immigrants, like myself, knew nothing, or very little, about their forebears, at least those forebears predating living relatives, save perhaps which country their distant ancestors likely came from. Currently there are those who comb genealogical records in order to unearth whatever information they can about their unknown forebears, with varying degrees of success.

Despite Kensington being heavily urbanized and ill-suited for a Thoreauvian nature walk, my walks nevertheless were able to deliver their own distinctive consolation for the soul. Long, solitary walks offered a welcome respite from the endless, obsessive rounds of athletic contests, such as stick ball, softball, handball, half ball, touch football, and three X's, played out on the hard concrete of the schoolyard of the local public school. In my case, that school was the Elkin Public School located at "D" and Clearfield Streets. In addition, the streets of Kensington, though deficient in greenery, are easily negotiated on foot. Most importantly, as far as my experience was concerned, these walks on Kensington streets took me back ceaselessly into the past, in consequence of the manifold traces in the environment of a past not immediately familiar. Thus, in this narrative, the timeline is not limited to memory.

My walks were consistent with Thoreau's injunction: "You must walk like a camel, which is said to be the only beast which ruminates while walking." The jaunt through Kensington featured in this narrative includes "ruminations." These ruminations focus attention upon a culture shaped by the immigrant communities which settled Kensington in the 19th century. The mills where immigrants worked and the churches which played a vital role in providing these communities with spiritual sustenance give testimony to the important contributions made by immigrants to the emergence of the United States as an economic powerhouse. While these arrivals from Europe did not always receive a friendly welcome from the native-born, their endurance paid dividends for their descendants. The trials undergone by those early waves of immigrants invite ruminations upon religion, race, education, and class. The contentiousness with which these issues are charged has never abated.

The "saunterer" featured in Thoreau's reflections had a sacred destination, by definition, according to his etymological theory. In my experience, a walk to downtown Philadelphia, where momentous events associated with the War of Independence took place, such as the promulgation of the Declaration of Independence and the tolling of the Liberty Bell, filled the bill as a trek to a hallowed destination. A walk from "D" Street in Upper Kensington—"D" Street just below Allegheny Avenue being the location of the residence where I grew up—all the way to downtown Philadelphia requires the traversing of the full length of Kensington. This is a journey of about three miles, ending at Girard Avenue. The journey can be accomplished in about twenty minutes by boarding the El at the Allegheny El station. But on foot one can meander, and this walk will be characterized by ample meandering in order to arouse all the ruminations that two centuries of Kensington history elicit. While the subjects of these ruminations include incidents and experiences which have transpired within living memory, the environment of Kensington, particularly that of Lower Kensington, stimulates reflection upon events from the distant past that have been little remembered. This narrative is part memoir, part historical record of important incidents in Kensington's history which predate living memory. It is a journey into the past as well as a journey through space.

The organizational logic of this book is structured around a walk. I begin, in Chapter 1, in the northernmost section of the neighborhood, where I grew up, and walk south, pointing out historical landmarks as I go. This structure may involve some disjunction to a reader who expects a more straightforward narrative which starts at the founding of Kensington and proceeds to the present day. In order to aid the reader in keeping his or her chronology straight, I have included a timeline in Appendix A. I feel that the geographical organization of this book, though a bit unusual, conforms to the kind of ambulatory adventures that I undertook in my youth. As my sauntering covered ground, I progressively entered into a past out of reach to living memory.

The final station of this ambulatory jaunt through Kensington is the shrine of Saint John Neumann, located at the southern extremity of Kensington at Saint Peter's church at 5th and Girard. It is a place to linger, where time stands still, and a place for reflection upon the life of a saint, whose body lies on view in a glass-enclosed reliquary before the altar of the lower church. While Neumann was bishop of Philadelphia, he requested to be laid to rest at Saint Peter's. The fulfillment of that request gave Kensington the proprietorship of a saint. Neumann had a preferential devotion to serving immigrant communities, and laid the groundwork for the parochial school system in Philadelphia. A biographical sketch of the saint will be included herein, followed by a reflection upon his legacy, consisting of an informal assessment of his sainthood as well as some commentary upon the educational system that he helped to launch and how it impacted generations of school children in Kensington. Hence, let this introduction stand as an invitation to the reader, whether a Kensington native like myself or a curious tourist, to walk along beside me during these saunterings and concomitant ruminations, if not to the Holy Land, then at least to places which may prove worthy of a pilgrimage.

PART I:

UPPER KENSINGTON

CHAPTER 1

A BRIEF GEOGRAPHICAL ORIENTATION

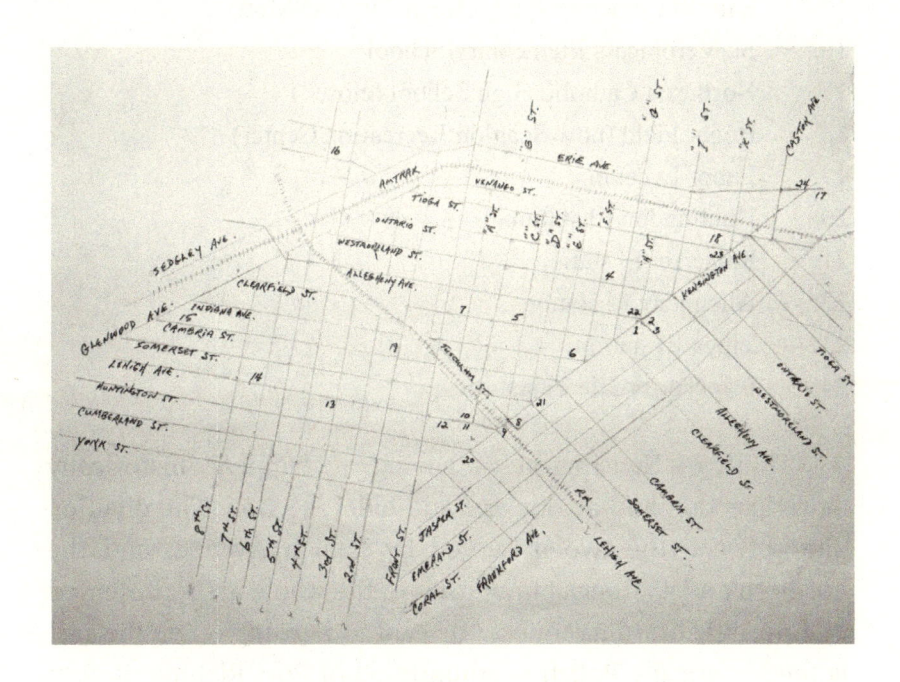

1. "K" & "A" (intersection of Kensington and Allegheny Avenues)
2. Horn & Hardart's restaurant & automat (closed)
3. Midway Theater (The Midway Theater was torn down in 1979)
4. Ascension church (closed in 2012)
5. "C" Street house (at 3115) trashed by racist mob
6. McPherson Square

7. Aberle Hosiery Mill (demolished)
8. Rocky Balboa house
9. Lehigh Viaduct
10. John Bromley and Sons textile mill (destroyed by fire)
11. Visitation Church
12. Episcopal Hospital
13. The Quaker Lace mill complex (destroyed by fire)
14. Northeast Public High School (later Thomas A. Edison High School) demolished
15. Fairhill Cemetery (gravesite of Lucretia Mott)
16. St. Veronica's Elementary School
17. Northeast Catholic High School (closed)
18. Boger Field (now Scanlon Recreation Center)
19. Labor Lyceum
20. Huntingdon El station
21. Somerset El station
22. Allegheny El station
23. Tioga El station
24. Erie-Torresdale El station

Think of Kensington as having an "upper," historically newer, section and a "lower," and older, section. The dividing line between the two is served by Lehigh Avenue, and the northern and southern boundaries of the whole are represented by Erie and Girard Avenues. Adjacent to Kensington on the east is the historically Polish neighborhood of Port Richmond, into which one enters upon crossing Aramingo Avenue. The western boundary of Kensington is a little more difficult to determine. To the west, Kensington faces what was in the past labelled, at least by whites, as the "black ghetto." Philadelphia has always been, and to some extent still is, a residentially segregated city. One proceeding in a westerly direction along Allegheny or Lehigh

Avenues notices a greater African-American presence the nearer one gets to Broad Street. Until at least the final decades of the twentieth century, residents of Kensington always considered their neighborhood strictly white. There was, in effect, a tacit understanding that whites belonged in their neighborhood and blacks belonged in theirs. Consequently, the daily lives of whites and blacks rarely intersected, except in the largely impersonal interactions that took place in the commercial world. It may be said, sadly, that in the minds of the white residents of Kensington, the western boundary of the neighborhood ran along the fault-line of wherever white residential streets ended and black residential streets began. While such a segregationist mentality prevailed through much of the 20th century, of late there has been some mitigation of the homogeneous whiteness of Kensington and considerable racial diversity is evident as one strolls along Kensington Avenue or Front Street. One element of the demographic transformation of Kensington over the past fifty or more years can be explained by the phenomenon of "white flight," which has impacted the urban landscape of Philadelphia extensively. But back in the 1950s, when one pushed west of Eighth or Ninth Streets, one was passing into the western fringes of Kensington and crossing, as it were, an informal though unmistakable color line.

CHAPTER 2

"K & A"

    The hub of Upper Kensington was, and is, the intersection of Kensington and Allegheny Avenues, colloquially referred to as "K and A." This fabled intersection avails as a fit launching pad for a walk through the length of Kensington. Serving to all in the neighborhood as the objective of going "down the avenue," the strip of Kensington Avenue extending south of Allegheny has lost a bit of its luster subsequent to post-industrial deterioration. Once featuring smart clothing shops, assorted retail stores such as hobby shops specializing in toy trains or tropical fish, bank branches, two movie theaters, drug stores with their popular soda fountains, a Horn and Hardart's eatery with its ever-popular automat, and a five and ten, the avenue is now home to convenience stores, pawn shops, dollar stores, and the inevitable spate of cellular phone outlets. Sunlight is at a premium as all on the avenue is situated beneath the metallic canopy of the el. Conspicuously missing in the current manifestation of K and A is the ever-smiling soft pretzel vender by the entrance to the el on the northeast corner of the intersection. That portable pretzel cart occupied what was certainly one of the most lucrative locations in the city, and the owner was the subject of a running joke that his humble pretzel cart had made him a millionaire.

A reference to K and A often elicits gasps of alarm, due to a long-standing perception of the area as a hub of criminal activity. Many decades ago, the larcenous activities of the gang that appropriated the K and A name were conducted without victimizing those of the local community. More bountiful pickings existed where the well-heeled resided, beyond the city limits. More recently, with the collapse of the manufacturing industry, the onset of demographic change brought on by white flight, and the upsurge of the popularity of crack and opioids, the dark side of Kensington is associated with the drug culture. The presence of bins on the street for the disposal of syringes serves as unmistakable evidence of a serious crisis afflicting present-day Kensington, particularly in the neighborhood of K and A.

CHAPTER 3

THE ASCENSION

What also cannot fail to be noticed in the vicinity of K and A is the Ascension. As much as the landscape of Upper Kensington is strewn here and there with mills of four or five stories, churches vie with them for prominence in the neighborhood's airspace. A short two-block walk along rowhouse-lined streets just west of K and A, the Ascension represented one of the largest Catholic parishes in the Archdiocese and figured prominently in the history of the neighborhood. This collection of buildings occupies the entire block bounded on the east and west by "F" and "G" Streets, and on the north and south by Cornwall and Westmoreland Streets. This extensive compound, consisting of a church building, two school buildings, a rectory, and a convent, is a rectangular island of large granite buildings surrounded by blocks and blocks of tightly-packed rowhouses. In terms of population, the Ascension represented one of the largest parish communities in the archdiocese. The area served by the parish was relatively small, but the population density was such that there was no need for school buses—everything was within walking distance. The thousand or so elementary school students enrolled at the Ascension lit out for school every morning on foot. The parish was established in 1899, and the two-tiered church (lower and upper church), with its red-tiled roof, colonnaded portico, and tall, gentle bell tower, could be gazed upon and admired from the windows of passing el trains several blocks to the east along Kensington Avenue. Currently the church is a deteriorating hulk, victim of the numerous church closures which have been carried out throughout the city over the past several decades by the archdiocese. The stained-glass windows and statuary have been removed and shipped out to other locations. Presumably, the church building has a date with the wrecking ball. Meanwhile, according to news reports, despite being boarded up and fenced off, it has been used as a shooting gallery and makeshift homeless shelter. Photos posted online a decade ago showed discarded syringes lying in dry marble holy water fonts. Needless to say, the elementary school, which comprised two school buildings, has closed shop as well. Currently, while the imposing structure which was the church stands in a state of degradation, other buildings on the campus have not gone unused. Occupying the building that served as the Ascension rectory is a Chinese evangelical Christian community, the name of the community being emblazoned in Chinese characters across the top of the building facade. Next door to the old rectory, the older of the two school buildings has been taken over by a Christian ministry known as Victory Outreach. The organization, which is international in scope, ministers to "the hurting people of the world," as its website announces.[1] In contemporary Kensington, "the hurting people of the world" seem to be well-represented.

If the clock may be turned back for a glimpse of the Ascension during its heyday as a populous Catholic parish, one would notice the figure of Father William Casey. He served there initially as a curate from 1914 to 1926. He was active in ministering to the sick and dying during the calamitous Spanish flu epidemic, which, in 1918, struck Philadelphia particularly hard as thousands of sailors passed through the city's navy yard upon returning from Europe after World War I. He was a serious baseball fan and an avid supporter of the Philadelphia Athletics. In 1923 he successfully recruited Babe Ruth to make a charity appearance at a semi-pro baseball game at Boger Field at "I" and Tioga Streets, a site secured by the Ascension at that time as a ball field. That field is currently occupied by the Scanlon Recreation Center.

The Babe spent much of his youth at a Catholic home for boys in Baltimore, where he was coached by one of the Catholic brothers to develop his baseball skills. The Babe lived hard, hit a baseball hard, and had a soft spot in his heart for kids and the Catholic Church. On Tuesday, September 4th, 1923, the New York Yankees came to town to play the Athletics at Shibe Park, where the game was scheduled to begin at 3:15pm. The amateur game was scheduled at Boger Field for 6:00 p.m., which was cutting it close. Thousands of fans were waiting there in anticipation. The Yankees pitcher, "Sad Sam" Jones, obliged by tossing a no-hitter. The game concluded in record time with a 2-

o Yankee victory. Upon being rushed up to the ball field in Kensington, the Babe donned the uniform of the Ascension team and took to the field as Ascension's first baseman. Ascension's opponent was a team fielded by the Lit Brothers department store, which, according to the *Philadelphia Inquirer*, was one of the strongest semi-pro teams in the city. Ruth had four at-bats. The first time up, he hit a ground-rule double (the ball being driven quite deep, it would have left Shibe Park, according to the news report), and he whacked two mile-high popups for outs. In his final at-bat, he reached second base on a fielding error and eventually scored Ascension's lone run in a 2-1 victory for Lit Brothers. At various moments between innings, Ruth tossed baseballs in the stands to kids with outreached hands and signed countless autographs. The stands were filled with ten thousand spectators and thousands more watched from nearby rowhouse rooftops and from the hillslope beyond the outfield leading up to the tracks of the Pennsylvania Railroad. Evident throughout the event was the joy that Ruth experienced in delighting his fans, especially those admiring youngsters.[2]

Casey was reassigned elsewhere in the archdiocese in 1926, but he returned as pastor of the Ascension in 1934, staying on in that capacity for the next several decades. He is best remembered by those who were active parishioners in the 1950s for his bilious philippics from the pulpit at Sunday masses, berating parishioners for their lack of generosity in the collection basket. That serious financial problems might have beset the parish at that time would not be surprising. With baby boomers entering grade school in the early 1950s, the Ascension school was bursting at the seams. There was a minimum of three classes per grade, and there were eight grades, and in each classroom there were between fifty and sixty students. A second school building was constructed and was ready for occupancy in 1954.

All of these students were enrolled tuition-free. Father Casey's tirades were not exactly benign requests for increased financial contributions—they were full-throated excoriations that had parishioners squirming in their pews. To small children he was Phineas T. Bluster, that grumpy, senescent character from the Howdy-Doody TV show. In one memorable diatribe, he reported to the congregation that he had found, at the bottom of the collection basket in the previous week's collection, a penny. "A penny!" he blared from the pulpit, his voice cracking with indignation.

By the end of the 1950s, a new pastor was assigned to the Ascension, and Father Casey stayed on as pastor emeritus. By that time, signs of an incipient dementia were evident. During the summer months he often said mass at the cramped convent chapel for the sisters who staffed the elementary school. I was often recruited to serve as altar boy at those masses, which were a bit of an adventure because the forgetful Father Casey would occasionally omit certain parts of the liturgy. After one mass, a visibly vexed sister approached me to ask: "Was there a consecration during the mass?" Adding to the ambiguity perhaps was the fact that the mass at the time was recited in Latin, often reeled off *sotto voce*, with the celebrant's back to the congregation. With dementia added to the mix, what precisely was going on could become even more uncertain.

Father Casey died in 1967. The moment was rich in turning points during a decade which represented a significant cultural watershed on many fronts. Demographic changes, which began in the 1950s, were in full swing. Kensingtonians were increasingly drawn to the suburbs, or to the so-called Great Northeast. Although within the city limits, the Northeast was unmistakably suburban to Kensingtonians due to the presence of that most quintessential feature of suburbia—the lawn. Baby boomers, groomed from the cradle to attend college, began accessing higher education by the mid-1960s and the vast majority of them would ultimately accede to the call of the suburbs. Concomitantly, the neighborhood grew increasingly Latino, largely Puerto Rican. The Ascension began scheduling masses in Spanish, just as parishes throughout Kensington were starting to do.

As the decade of the seventies began, the Ascension school, along with other parochial schools in the archdiocese, announced that it would no longer be capable of fulfilling the hundred-year old pledge to offer tuition-free Catholic education to parish children. With decreasing numbers of sisters available to staff the school, parochial schools needed to hire more and more lay teachers, who, unlike the sisters with their vow of poverty, required a living wage. Needless to say, the tuition, relatively low at first, predictably increased over time and grew out of reach to a demographic ill-equipped to shoulder such a big financial burden. Enrollment declined, and the Ascension elementary school eventually closed.

Like many parishes in Kensington, the Ascension served its parishioners in its heyday by not only functioning in its liturgical and devotional roles, but also by fulfilling a role as a community center. In regard to the former, the daily calendar of the church was filled to overflowing. Masses on Sunday were scheduled virtually on the hour from 6:00 a.m. to noon. At certain hours there would be two masses scheduled simultaneously—one in the upper church, and one in the lower. On weekdays and Saturdays, there were three masses scheduled between the hours of 5:00 a.m. and 8:00 a.m.. A typical Saturday morning often saw more than one nuptial mass celebrated, except during the penitential seasons of Advent and Lent. As there are no liturgical seasons during which death takes a break, nary a week went by during the year without several funerals Monday through Saturday. It is perhaps the Requiem Mass that most dramatically demonstrates the liturgical changes ushered in since the 1960s. Prior to the Second Vatican Council, the funeral liturgy was celebrated in accordance with centuries-old practice, that is, liturgical practice prescribed by the Council of Trent in the 16th century. Black vestments were worn by the celebrant of a requiem mass, as well as by the deacon and the subdeacon in the event of a solemn requiem mass. The cassocks worn by the altar servers were also black. The *Dies Irae* was intoned in Latin—indeed, the funeral mass was entirely celebrated in Latin. Numerous supplications were offered to God calling for mercy upon the soul of the deceased. The mystery of death was ceremoniously evoked throughout the liturgy. After all, the existential status of the deceased remained rather shrouded in mystery. At the same time the theological virtue of hope pervaded the liturgy. That proclamation of hope was what provided solace to mourners and which strengthened them in trusting in the promises of Christ. That is to say, hope is the theological virtue which is the mean between despair, on the one hand, and presumption, on the other.

Since the 1960s, white vestments have replaced the black, the *Dies Irae* has been discarded, and it is not unusual to hear from the celebrant those comforting words to the effect that the deceased is now enjoying eternal bliss in Heaven. Be that as it may (or not), the virtue of hope seems often to be underplayed currently, in favor of a note of what smacks of presumption. Thus is evoked the notion of assurance of salvation which has characterized the faith of certain Protestant sects. It may be said that if salvation of one's soul is believed to be obtainable prior to death—in the here and now—then there is no need for hope, as the prize is already won in the midst of life. Hope is not necessarily an easy virtue, and a brief rumination on that topic is not unwarranted.

The state of fear, particularly as it relates to mortality, uniquely disposes those afflicted by that emotion to be eminently exploitable. "Be not afraid" is a counsel expressed prominently in the Gospels. It is a counsel that has not always been promoted by the Church hierarchy in its manner of shepherding the faithful. That is to say, there was gold in the fears of the faithful. Among the many abuses wrought by the Church, i.e., the hierarchy of the Church, was the practice in the Middle Ages of offering the faithful a means whereby they could mitigate their fear of death, and fulfill their hope that eternal bliss in Heaven would follow death, by purchasing indulgences. The Church could thereby fill its coffers while the faithful could feel comforted that their time in Purgatory would be shortened and their entry into Heaven expedited. Fear of death, like any fear only more so, is eminently exploitable.

When the Protestant Reformers justly called out this abuse represented by the sale of indulgences and launched the Protestant Reformation, they proceeded to generate a variety of theological proposals about the process of salvation, that is, the process of how entry into eternal life in Heaven can be secured. One such theological formulation placed emphasis upon God's absolute otherness, omnipotence, and omniscience, to the point that seemed to lead logically to the doctrine of predestination. God's omniscience, so the doctrine dictated, foreordained the postmortem destiny of all creatures, so there is nothing on the part of human beings that can be done to earn God's favor or to alter what has already been determined. Whatever the fine nuances of the Reformers' understanding of the theological doctrine of predestination may have been, the average believer, predictably, zeroed in on the distinction between those predestined to be saved and those predestined to eternal damnation. The question became not so much how one should order one's life in order to conform to the teachings of the Gospels, but how to ascertain if one is registered among the saved. Thus there are religious sects in which the community professes the conviction that its members have assurance of salvation in the here and now in the midst of life at little or no apparent cost. For those beset by an overweening desire for certainty and assurance, such a conviction would seem to dispense with the theological virtue of hope. Perhaps such a conviction or feeling of assurance can provide some insulation from the slough of despair and anxiety, but it does so at the cost of the sort of hope that the New Testament counsels: "For in this hope we were saved. But hope that is seen is no hope at all. Who hopes for what they already have? But if we hope for what we do not yet have, we wait for it patiently." (Romans: 24-25)

Our world offers unlimited reasons for despair. For that reason, hope is not an easy virtue. The future may often look dark, but the disciple of Christ takes sustenance from the promises of Christ as set forth in the Gospels. Evangelical hope sustains the believer in the Gospels in the face of all the compelling reasons to succumb to despair.

However often it is now heard at a Catholic funeral mass that the deceased is enjoying eternal bliss in Heaven, Catholics still send mass cards, prayers are still offered for the dead, and God's mercy is still beseeched for the soul of the deceased. All Soul's Day is still celebrated on November 2nd when all of the deceased are prayed for so that God may welcome them into Heaven. The observance of the practice of praying for the dead—a practice commended in Chapter 12 of the second book of the Maccabees—would seem to be appropriate, since judgments about any person's post-mortem destiny are something solely lying within the province of God. Mortals are not the ones to render judgments about the fate of the souls of one's fellow mortals. There are those officially recognized by the Church, through the exacting process of canonization, as being with God in Heaven and who, by virtue of this status, are able to intercede with God for us. According to Catholic belief, the Saints are venerated owing to saintly and heroic deeds in life, and they can be prayed to as intercessors with God on our behalf.

To round out the array of religious activities at the Ascension besides daily masses, funerals, and weddings, there was a wealth of communal devotional activities celebrated, some of which might be deemed representative of old-world piety. These included novenas, parish missions, Stations of the Cross, benediction of the Blessed Sacrament, forty-hour devotions, communal rosary recitation, and the annual May procession. The recitation of the Angelus prayer—three times daily: 6:00 a.m., 12noon, and 6:00 p.m.—was among other devotions frequently practiced at that time.

The custom of women being "churched" was commonly observed, whereby a woman who had recently given birth presented herself at the altar rail before the priest for a special blessing, usually following one of the weekday morning masses. The rite essentially honored the major life event of childbirth in a woman's life, offering both thanksgiving as well as an invocation for the well-being of the newborn. While the ceremonious recognition of a life-changing event such as childbirth would seem entirely appropriate and salutary, the ceremony was seen by some in a negative light, as a kind of purification rite, on the grounds that the experiences of conception, pregnancy, and childbirth were somehow considered to be "unclean" and hence the ceremonious "cleansing" represented by the rite sanctioned the re-introduction of the new mother back into the church community. Since the 1960s, the rite has been infrequently practiced.

The community life fostered by the Ascension included a wide range of activities, not simply overtly religious ones. There were dances, game nights, weekly bingo, and educational presentations on manifold topics. There were organizations such as the Holy Name Society, the Knights of Columbus, the St. Vincent de Paul Society, various ladies' sodalities—all of which served social ends besides just spiritual ones. Foot traffic in the vicinity of the Ascension always abounded.

The Ascension Elementary School merits further discussion as generations of the children of Catholic families in Upper Kensington received their education there. Opening in 1900, the school experienced soaring enrollments during the 1950s and 1960s as the baby boom generation reached school-age. A photograph of my 1960 eighth grade class shows sixty pupils—a class which was just one of three eighth grade classes of comparable size. It should be noted that there was no middle school—parochial elementary schools in the city consisted of eight grades, and all classes were coed. The teachers assigned the responsibility to manage these large classes resided in the adjacent convent, as they were members of the religious community known as the Sisters of Saint Joseph. The sisters took their vocation as educators of children very seriously. Central to the education provided was the Catholic faith, which was taught during the daily religion class hour, but which suffused the entire curriculum. It may be said that their religious commitment was acknowledged without reservation. Living in community in accordance with the evangelical vows of poverty, chastity, and obedience and attired in their religious habit, the sisters manifested their religious commitment by virtue of the life they had chosen. Theirs was no empty profession of faith, in contrast with those who profess the Christian faith but whose professed religious beliefs are often little reflected in actual daily behavior.

The class routine, as well as the iconography of the classroom, bespoke two fundamental values—Christian faith and good citizenship. The morning kicked off with a prayer, normally a formulaic prayer such as the Our Father or the Hail Mary, recited before the visage of the suffering Christ, a crucifix being prominently affixed on the front wall of every classroom. The Pledge of Allegiance followed, recited with hand over heart facing the American flag, also positioned prominently in the front of the class.

While the formative impact of teachers is a matter beyond question, it has always been a popular pastime to reminisce about certain peculiarities of the instruction provided in the typical Ascension classroom. There is no question about the high quality of the education delivered there—an impressive feat, considering the average class size of around sixty students per class. Some of the anecdotes shared by teachers with the class were charged with much religious piety and often taxed credibility, but there is no point in detracting from the undeniable dedication of the sisters to their vocation. Any exception to this only serves to prove the rule. It would serve little purpose to recall such memorable anecdotes presented in class such as the one about a woman, a non-Catholic and a beekeeper by trade. This woman heard that bees derive some nutritional benefit from the unleavened bread that constitutes the hosts used during Catholic Mass. She attended a Mass and upon receiving the host in communion, surreptitiously removed it from her mouth and deposited it in her purse. When she introduced the host into the hive, she was astounded to observe that the bees arrayed themselves reverently around the host, while their buzzing resonated with the melody of the Tantum Ergo, the Latin hymn intoned during Benediction of the Blessed Sacrament.

Nor would any particular benefit derive from recounting the story of the student, who, sometime in the distant past, unwisely struck one of the sisters. The hapless student, it was reported, suffered the loss of the offending right arm later in an accident—victim of an obvious and, seemingly, well-deserved act of divine retribution. The lesson of the story was immediately transparent, although it must be pointed out that battery on the part of students against teachers was virtually unknown.

Class discipline was given a high priority, and the sisters were highly skilled at maintaining order, which, given the average class size of sixty students, was an invaluable skill. There were some teachers, though very few in number, who did not eschew the use of corporal punishment when an incident of unruliness erupted. One sister notoriously kept a wooden chair leg in a drawer of the teacher's desk. The implement was well-nigh two feet in length and inexplicably dubbed "percy." A miscreant being caught talking out of order in class would be summoned to the front of the class, and, the location of "percy" being familiar to all, would be required to remove it from the desk drawer and hand it to the teacher. Bending forward against the side of the teacher's desk, the student would be inflicted with a dozen loud whacks to the behind. While the pain was intensely palpable and one's behind would be marked with red welts lasting several days, such pain did not compare with the humiliation at being walloped before the eyes of the entire class. Only boys would be subject to the discipline exacted by "percy," unless some intrapsychic mechanism has operated to bury what would be too disturbing a memory, that of a female classmate being similarly whacked. Upon further reflection, there were other anatomical parts not exempt from being afflicted with whacks, such as the upturned palm of the outstretched arm—the whacks being meted out by a flexible ruler. Girls were not immune from that mortification, and the pain thereby inflicted more than sufficed.

When it came to the learning content which prevailed in class, it may be said that the contours of all of life's antinomies were starkly drawn—good and evil, right and wrong, true and false, all of which binary contrasts, it may be conceded, did not fail to conform with the cognitive stage of pre-adolescent learners. Subtleties, nuances, and shades of gray would come with later cognitive development. The standard of virtue and Christian practice was represented in the example provided by the saints, while a distinct rogues gallery featured embodiments of wickedness, such as Karl Marx, whose aphorism, "religion is the opium of the people," was sufficient, without the necessity of any analysis of his theories, to qualify him for condemnation. Those deemed as heretics were demonized. Prominently featured in the catalogue of propagators of theological error was Martin Luther. It would not be until after the Second Vatican Council that Luther's anthem, "A Mighty Fortress," would find its way into the Catholic hymnal—lyrics seriously altered, of course. The greatest perpetrator of treason was Benedict Arnold, a particularly dastardly traitor since among the reasons he gave to claim justification for his betrayal of the country was his disapproval of America's alliance, during the War of Independence, with France, "the enemy of the Protestant faith."

Finally, another figure who deserves mention as someone who was consistently demonized in the parochial elementary school classroom such as that of the Ascension is the American philosopher and educational reformer John Dewey. Dewey wrote prolifically on the topic of pedagogy and his ideas carried much weight throughout the 20th century in teacher-training programs. A proponent of "progressive education," Dewey advocated a "child-centered" classroom. He objected to traditional teaching methods whereby the teacher simply lays out material for the student to pack away mentally. Rote learning had little place in his system. Dewey's pedagogy was based upon the premise that children learn through experience. The teacher's role is not to fill the child's mind with information but to foster a learning environment in which the child actively participates in the process of learning. Dewey's writings evoked the Emersonian manifesto: "The foregoing generations beheld God and nature face-to-face; we, through their eyes. Why should not we also enjoy an original relation to the universe? Why should not we have a poetry and philosophy of insight and not of tradition, and a religion by revelation to us, and not the history of theirs?"[3] Inherited traditions and creeds are not only desiccated, to his mind, but have been incrementally discredited due to modern advances in scientific understanding which provide empirically-based accounts of natural phenomena—accounts which have thereby debunked, for example, Scripturally-based accounts of the origins of life, such as those contained in the book of Genesis. The Ascension Elementary School classroom, in which the vast majority of the teachers were Catholic sisters trained in Catholic universities, could not accommodate such a pedagogical vision. In the parochial elementary school classroom, the magisterium of the Church, as the repository of timeless truths, represented the ultimate authority when it came to what is real and true. The teacher's role was to bequeath this deposit of truth to young minds. Dewey, who identified himself as a secular humanist, was not in sympathy with church-affiliated schools, and envisioned no future for religion, at least as it was traditionally understood and practiced. The products of a school like the Ascension might little remember John Dewey, but if they do, they are probably saddled with very negative associations related to the relentlessly vilified theorist.

Equally memorable were those school days when a class would be marched to the local movie theater—the Midway at K & A—in order to view a religiously-themed film. One such memorable occasion featured the film, "The Miracle of Our Lady of Fatima." In a welcome respite from the usual daily routine, pupils would be marched on a weekday afternoon several blocks to the Midway in uniform columns. The sisters had unmatched skill at imposing regimentation. The film debuted in the 1950s, and packed a punch, at least to an audience consisting of 9, 10, or 11-year-old children. The protagonists of the film, three similarly-aged children growing up in humble circumstances, make an immediate connection with that young audience. The locale is the village of Fatima in rural Portugal during the era of World War I. While out in the fields one day in 1916 tending sheep, the three children—Lúcia, age 10, and her two slightly younger cousins, Francisco and Jacinta— experience a vision of an angel enjoining them to pray for peace and for the salvation of sinners, and requests that they return to the same site once every month for further communications. Francisco initially is prevented from seeing the vision, which was in no way surprising to the audience since boys are naughtier and less virtuous than girls, as everyone knew, and hence less predisposed than girls to incur religious experiences. Further angelic apparitions follow. Then on May 13th, 1917, a beautiful lady bathed in a brilliant light appeared before the children and counseled them to pray for peace. The children's enthusiastic reports of their visions are not well received back in the village, and as the news spreads, the children are afflicted with recriminations and threats. It so happens that at the time, Portugal was in the midst of a wave of anti-clericalism and a secularizing policy was being implemented by the government bent upon placing extensive restrictions upon the power of the Church. Political authorities, fearful of a groundswell of religious fervor among the peasantry brought about by the children's claims, attempt to silence the children with offers of bribes. When that fails, they threaten physical punishment, including threats of death. All the while the guileless children remain stubbornly refractory to all attempts by the authorities, including Church authorities, who are eager to placate government officials, to impel them to disavow their visions. The children continue to defy authority by returning to the site of the appearances of Mary, the Mother of God, as the lady identifies herself. The children are told to expect a sign—a miracle—as evidence to the world that the apparitions which the children are witnessing are real. As the children report this latest message received from the lady, the country is thrown into a state of frenzy. Humble peasants await the promised miracle in a state of religious excitement, while imperious government officials and equally imperious Church authorities await what they expect will be the inevitable failure of the miracle to materialize. The children will thus be exposed as attention-seeking frauds and all the disruptive fakery will end. As tens of thousands of people gather on a cloudy day on the assigned date at the site of the children's visions, the crowd does indeed get the miracle—and with a vengeance. The sun emerges from behind a cloud, spinning wildly and throwing off a dizzying kaleidoscope of colors, while steadily expanding in size as if careening toward the earth on a collision course. The crowd is thrown into a state of panic before what seems like the imminent end of the world. The episode lasts several minutes and by the time the sky resolves into its familiar guise, all skepticism towards the children's claims has been swept away in one stroke.

If the gratifying deflation of the arrogance of the adult world by three simple children not yet in their teens was not dramatic enough, there was still more drama to come. In a follow-up commentary on the film, it was reported that the lady, the Mother of God, entrusted the children with three "secrets" or visions with prophetic impact, and of momentous import to the world. Lúcia, the oldest of the three children, revealed this in a memoir composed by her decades later. The first so-called secret featured a vision of hell, and it was a vision that conceded nothing to the faint of heart nor to those inclined to downplay the horrifying cogency of hell. Hell is essentially a deep pit in which a roaring, unquenchable conflagration rages, from which emanates a cacophony of wails and groans and an unrelenting stench of putrescence. Amid the flames and clouds of smoke could be seen a grotesquerie of howling, gnarled demons and the smoldering souls of the human dead consigned to hell for all eternity. Alarmingly, souls of the newly-deceased were seen continuously falling into this raging inferno "like snowflakes during a snowstorm." Only repentance, the Lady warns, can curb this loss of souls.

The second secret featured the prediction of the impending end to World War I—the revelation was made in 1917—and the prediction of an even more cataclysmic world war in the future unless humankind turns to God in prayer and makes repentance for the world's sins.

The mysterious third secret was sealed away and the revelation of its contents was scheduled for the year 1960. The Cold War being in full swing during the 1950s and the conviction among many at that time that World War III was imminent, speculation ran rampant over what the third secret might portend. The most apocalyptic scenarios were imagined in a decade characterized by an unremitting arms race, featuring nuclear weapons, between the U.S.S.R. and the United States, the building of fallout shelters, and the exercise of random, unannounced air raid drills to insure readiness for the inevitable real McCoy. In 1960, the Vatican, which was in possession of the sealed envelope containing the secret, refrained from disclosing its contents. Reportedly, Pope John XXIII, upon reading the prophecy, determined that it was not expedient to comment on the third secret at that time. Predictably, many speculated that what the third secret revealed was so horrific that the Pope settled for silence over the possibility of provoking worldwide panic. It was not until the Papacy of Benedict XVI that it was disclosed that the third secret involved the prediction of the assassination attempt on the life of Pope John Paul II on May 13th, 1981. This was a particularly dispiriting anti-climactic revelation, especially since the attempt on John Paul's life, however deplorable, failed anyway. There were those, however, who saw unearthly significance in the fact that the incident took place on the same day in May—the 13th—when Mary first appeared to the three children in Fatima. If the suspense generated by the "three secrets" has subsided, Fatima remains a much-visited and hallowed place of pilgrimage.

By mid-century, graduates of the Ascension were moving on to high school as a matter of course. A brief flashback provides the background for the emergence of the high school for children of Kensington families. During the era when Kensington was known as the "workshop of the world," it was taken for granted that education beyond elementary school for Kensington residents was superfluous—local industry required thousands of workers and supplied all the employment needs that could be imagined for the residents of Kensington. By the end of the 19th century, overtures for more education were beginning to be made. This initiative was driven by virtue of higher expectations on the part of the descendants of immigrant families for their children and also because of the work of child welfare advocates who inveighed against the child labor practices of the 19th and early 20th centuries. Activists like Mother Jones tirelessly went public about the hazardous conditions and long working hours endured by children in mills and mines. Her "March of the Mill Children" in 1903 was launched on July 7th from the Labor Lyceum at 2nd and Cambria Streets in Kensington. Children bearing placards with rallying cries such as "We want to go to school" and "We only ask for Justice" were bound for President Theodore Roosevelt's summer home on Long Island, New York.

The Archdiocese responded to the growing desire on the part of elementary school graduates for secondary education by opening the Northeast Catholic High School for boys in 1926, located on Torresdale Avenue in the extreme northeast corner of Kensington hard by the Erie-Torresdale El station. In 1939, the Little Flower High School for girls opened its doors in the Hunting Park neighborhood. North Catholic drew students from various neighborhoods in North Philadelphia. During the years following World War II, soaring enrollments exceeding 4,500 students necessitated the use of several annexes at Kensington parishes for freshman classes. While North Catholic closed in 2010 after several decades of declining enrollments, Little Flower has remained in business.

Before resuming this walk through Upper Kensington, it may be added that, needless to say, church and school closures in recent decades have left post-industrial Kensington with only a handful of parochial elementary schools. Besides the Visitation school on Lehigh Avenue and that of St. Peter's parish on Girard Avenue, St. Veronica's Elementary School at 6th and Venango Streets in the northwest corner of Kensington has also survived.

St. Veronica's opened in 1894, and has a lengthy history. The school's website describes the current manifestation of the school as "an independence mission school." An elementary school with a much shorter history is the LaSalle Academy, which opened in 2003 in a former convent on 2nd Street across from St. Michael's church. Offering six grades of elementary education from third grade to eighth, the school maintains a census of between ninety and one hundred students. These contemporary schools serve a much more racially and ethnically diverse population of students than the schools like the Ascension, of yesteryear Kensington.

CHAPTER 4

THE STREET LIFE OF UPPER KENSINGTON: A REMINISCENCE

While the street life of the K & A neighborhood was enlivened by the Ascension's students heading to school or North Catholic students heading to the Allegheny el station, such did not exhaust the wellsprings of activity and bristling foot traffic that contributed to the bustle of Upper Kensington. Families tended to be large, often consisting of six, seven, or more children, and on the streets were frequently staged impromptu athletic contests or other diversions such as hide-and-seek, tag, dodge ball, and the like. An ice cream truck trolling the neighborhood in the summer blaring out a catchy jingle drew legions of children into the streets clamoring for a popsicle or frozen fudge bar. Hucksters from Jersey truck farms loudly hawking fresh produce—tomatoes, corn, peppers, melons, blueberries—summoned housewives into the streets. Assorted entrepreneurs, such as those vending pony rides, plied the streets with pony in tow. Warm weather brought residents out to sit on their front steps or on aluminum folding chairs, often listening to the play-by-play of Phillies' games on transistor radios. Such never-say-die fans persisted in their loyalty, in spite of the Phillies' tendency to engender heartbreak.

Charles Lutz

Despite the Phillies' long history, dating from 1883, the team did not win a World Series championship until 1980. They hold the record for the highest number of losses, overall, of any major league baseball franchise. In 1961, they suffered a losing streak of twenty-three games. This losing streak still stands as a major league record. They have a reputation for late-season collapses. Most notable was the epic collapse in 1964, when, having spent the entire season in first place and entering the month of September with a six and a half game lead, they proceeded to lose ten games in a row and were edged out for the National League pennant by the St. Louis Cardinals on the last day of the season. Inured to disappointment, Phillies fans likely acquired their reputation for boorishness owing to their being afflicted with unending woe.

If Kensington in the mid-20th century was felt by many of its residents to be a locale where events of momentous import to the world were uncommon, there was nevertheless a bit of excitement that unfolded on the night of September 30th, 1960. A commotion was reported on the evening news that was taking place on the 3100 block of "C" Street. Without attempting to learn more about the exact nature of the ruckus and being simply driven by curiosity, I determined to travel one block to the west of "D" Street to check out a rare newsworthy event. In the encroaching twilight, a large crowd could be seen gathered mid-block before one of the non-descript rowhomes. The mood was festive and celebratory, suggestive of a block party, but it quickly became clear that what was being celebrated had a destructive and malevolent design. From the midst of the crowd, rocks were being flung in the direction of the house in succession, and as each projectile smashed into the house, breaking its windows and marring the façade, loud, jubilant cheers were elicited. Racist epithets were emblazoned across the red brick exterior of the house, and were scrawled as well on placards held aloft, not only by adults in the mob but also by young children. What was on display was a mob-driven hate crime, organized to prevent a young African-American family from taking residence on the all-white block. The scene was a shocking revelation to a young, pre-adolescent mind. The mob was sizable, numbering well into the hundreds, but if my family received the memo, I was not aware of it.

There was a significant police presence on the street, but no attempt on the part of the police was made to interfere with the vandalism. Then one policeman who was wielding a bullhorn requested the attention of the mob and proceeded to deliver the message that the family had reconsidered its plans and would not be taking up residence in the house after all. While the announcement elicited an immediate roar of jubilation and a round of high-fives, the mob did not disperse, as many were overtaken by a sense of suspicion. The police thereupon decided to call upon the services of the pastor of the Ascension—a Father Charles Mallon, successor to Father Casey—to give assurance to the crowd that the block would remain uniformly white. Furnished with the *de rigeur* bullhorn, Mallon successfully convinced the crowd that they could confidently disperse with the knowledge that they had achieved their objective.

No report of the incident can be found in the October 1st, 1960 edition of the Philadelphia Inquirer, but the Philadelphia Tribune, the local African-American paper, features a front-page rundown under the banner headline, "Little Children Carried Hate Signs in Kensington Mob."[4]

In the account of the incident, the rabble is described as consisting of about 700 participants. Supplementing the account of the incident are two images—one showing the trashed rowhome, the other a portrait of the four-member Harris family which had been poised to take up residence in the "C" Street rowhouse. Mr. and Mrs. Ernest Harris are shown with their two children, Reuben, age 4, and Stephen, age 2. All four with smiling faces, the images are featured under the heading, "Smiling after the Ordeal." In the accompanying report Mr. Harris indicates his disinclination to place his family in jeopardy, and expresses disappointment with the police. Perhaps what is most difficult to ignore is that which is featured in the headline—the image of young children carrying "hate signs." Presumably, some parents saw the incident as an occasion for an educational moment with a view to instilling in their children the basics of the disposition of racism. Thus was demonstrated the claim put forth by one of the characters of the popular film of the Rodgers and Hammerstein musical, *South Pacific*, which appeared in movie theaters two years earlier in 1958: "Racism is not born in you; it happens after you're born." The deliverer of that line, Lt. Cable, thereupon bursts into the song, "You've Got to Be Carefully Taught," in which it is proclaimed that children must be "carefully" nurtured to "hate and fear" those who have different physical characteristics from theirs, such as a different skin color. Such education, the song continues to insist, must be carried out "before it is too late", while the young mind is still tractable. The irony would be funny if it did not describe such an exploitative program to recruit the young into a hate cult.

While the children bearing placards were being recruited by their parents into an educational practicum as part of their training for racism, the Harris children—Reuben and Stephen—likewise were treated to a demonstration of what they could expect for their future in a society afflicted with intergenerational, systemic racism. Those driven by curiosity to witness this dispiriting event were left to reflect upon their voyeurism and upon disturbing questions such as: *How many of the children and their parents participating in the event were students of and products of the Ascension where a central feature of the curriculum were the values embodied in the Gospels?* As is so often the case with such odious incidents, the ingenious ability of human beings to construct rationalizations for abhorrent behavior was put on view, such as that it was deemed necessary to protect the neighborhood from crime or protect property values from depreciating. Some speculated that the incident represented an attempt on the part of realtors to conduct a blockbusting scheme—the custom whereby realtors provoke panic and a flurry of home sales in a predominantly white neighborhood by generating the fear that the neighborhood is about to be taken over by non-whites. As it was, however, the phenomenon of "white flight" was about to take off and alter the demographic makeup of Kensington in a profound way.

CHAPTER 5

MCPHERSON SQUARE

Heading back in the direction of Kensington Avenue, one encounters the sylvan retreat known as McPherson Square at the corner of "E" and Clearfield Streets. In the center of square stands a dignified neoclassical edifice serving as a branch of the Free Library of Philadelphia. If it is true, as Thoreau stated, that in reference to nature, "we need the tonic of wildness," residents of Kensington would need to make do with the greenery, however lacking in wildness, that McPherson Square offered.

McPherson Square takes its name from General William McPherson, a Revolutionary War general who constructed a country home on the site where the current library building stands, and who occasionally hosted George Washington in his mansion. The mansion eventually passed into the possession of a prominent family named Webster. In 1898 the mansion and grounds were purchased by the city of Philadelphia and the McPherson branch of the Free Library of Philadelphia was dedicated, opening in the old Webster estate.

Construction of a new building began in 1915, replacing the old mansion with a domed Palladium villa with a colonnaded portico. The library was a popular haunt for children in the 1950s and 1960s, and likely still is, at least for those who like to read. But as deindustrialization, unemployment rates, and the exodus to the suburbs have accelerated, the square has turned into a gathering place for those involved in the drug culture. According to news reports, during the first decade of the 21st century, the square devolved into a hub of the heroin epidemic, earning it the nickname, "Needle Park." Discourse related to the square has included the familiar phenomena—discarded syringes littering the ground, the occasional fatal overdose, and police indifference to the deterioration of the square. Eventually, greater media attention brought about some action to clean up the square and attend to what can only be called a serious health crisis.

By the second decade of the 21st century, librarians at the library were being trained to administer the nasal spray Narcan to those suffering respiratory depression consequent to an opioid overdose, according to news reports. At the same time, bins have been installed on the sidewalks around the square for the disposal of used syringes. Thus has the square been serving as a depressing barometer of the devolution of society, insofar as the job description of librarians now includes the ability to administer Narcan.

Visitors to the park, whether in the mid-20th century or more recently, probably have failed to attend to the presence in the park, hard by the steps leading up to the entrance to the library, of a granite pedestal topped by an erect human figure. The figure is that of Charles Allen Smith, whose story has been recovered from oblivion by the online historian Bob McNulty, who operates a website devoted to the history of Philadelphia, with particular emphasis upon the history of Kensington.[5] The 20-year-old Smith, reared in Kensington, was a US Navy seaman killed in 1914 in a military operation conducted in Mexico. Prior to the entry of the United States into World War I in 1917, the United States had been at the brink of war with Mexico, whose revolution between 1910-1920 placed American economic interests there at risk. Determined to protect US interests,

President Woodrow Wilson dispatched the battleship U.S.S. New Hampshire to the east coast of Mexico. Smith was assigned to that battleship. In an act of perhaps unwise and needless bravado, Wilson ordered the occupation of Vera Cruz. Smith was one member of a landing party consisting of upwards of 500 marines and 300 sailors. The operation achieved its objective, but Smith was fatally struck by a sniper's bullet. Smith's body, along with that of another casualty from Philadelphia, lay in state on the morning of May 13th, 1914 at Independence Hall where over half a million paid their respects. In the afternoon, a funeral procession bore Smith's body to Kensington on E. Sergeant Street, where Smith's grieving mother struggled to contain her grief, passing in and out of consciousness as the casket bearing her son was delivered to the house.

During the ensuing years, residents of Kensington determined to erect a memorial to the fallen sailor, and the monument in MacPherson Square was dedicated in 1917. Over 10,000 paid tribute at the dedication ceremony at MacPherson Square, according to McNulty's chronicle. The passage of time dimmed the memory of Smith and the monument began serving as an attractive surface for graffiti artists. Happily, of late, the monument has been spruced up and stands with its original luster.

McPherson Square continued to serve in its role as a setting for momentous community events during the first half of the 20th century, when labor strife broke out in Kensington during the depression years. It should come as no surprise that Kensington, as the locus of so much industry, played a significant part in the growth of labor unions. The Knights of Labor was founded in 1869 by Uriah Stephens during a meeting that took place in a rowhouse on the 2300 block of Coral Street, several blocks to the east of where the York-Dauphin el station now stands.

Needless to say, labor unions were not popular with the business magnates of the textile industry in Kensington, and unions operated rather cautiously during the early decades of their existence. When the Great Depression descended upon the industry after the economic collapse of 1929, management began imposing severe restrictions on wages, and unions became emboldened to act.

Early in 1930, workers of the Aberle Hosiery mill at "A" and Clearfield Streets went on strike. The mill employed over 1,000 workers and, following the work stoppage, the owners offered employment to whomever was willing to cross the picket line, that is, to that most hated of blackguards in the annals of Kensington history, the scab. A hosiery worker named Carl Mackley, though a member of a separate hosiery union, showed solidarity with the Aberle mill workers by joining their picket line. On March 6th, 1930, tension between the picketers and the scabs was nearing a fever pitch. When the strike-breaking workers ended their workday at 5:00 p.m. and proceeded from the factory escorted by the police through crowds of angry picketers, several carloads of strikers prepared to follow them. Mackley was an occupant of one of the cars in the caravan of strike-breakers' vehicles with their police escort. The strikers' vehicles advanced northward along Front Street. When the vehicles crossed Erie Avenue, the police escort turned off. Thereupon ensued a dangerous game whereby the sparring vehicles attempted to force one another off the road. At one point, a strikebreaker's car stopped at a red light. Mackley's vehicle pulled alongside and its occupants began flinging projectiles at the strikebreaker's car. Perhaps unbeknownst to the strikers, the occupants of the strikebreaker's car were armed, and once the windshield of their car was shattered, they retaliated by unleashing a hail of bullets at the strikers' vehicle. Each of the occupants of the striker's car were hit. Mackley was fatally struck in the head, while the other three suffered wounds that were not life-threatening. Mackley became immediately hailed as a martyr in the cause of labor rights, and was honored with a memorial service held at McPherson Square several days after the incident.[6] Over 30,000 paid homage to the fallen hosiery worker.

Notably, the conflict between the striking workers and management went to arbitration the following April and the union emerged with their demands having been successfully met. The four strikebreakers, none of whom were residents of Kensington, did not avoid prosecution. It was determined that the fatal bullet was fired by a strikebreaker named William Pfeiffer. The case against Pfeiffer went to trial the following May and the jury found him to be not guilty by virtue of self-defense. While Pfeiffer's court victory was gratifying for the defendant, his life remained in sufficient danger that he found it expedient to relocate out of state. He lived out the remainder of his life in Tennessee, as reported by the Public Ledger.

Several years later, McPherson Square again discharged its role as a setting for momentous community events serving as the site for a protest aiming to deny passage of "Open Sunday" laws.[7] Advocates of "Open Sunday" laws sought a lifting of restrictions on a variety of activities not legally permitted on Sundays—laws enacted in the 1790s.

Most notable of these restricted activities were professional sports games. A central target of the opponents of the "Open Sundays" policy was Connie Mack, owner and manager of the Philadelphia Athletics, who had successfully wrangled an exemption for baseball several years earlier that enabled the legendary manager to schedule Athletics' games on Sundays at Shibe Park.

Another local sports magnate, one Bert Bell, was in the midst of attempting to put together a professional football franchise in Philadelphia, and was agitating for a repeal of the Pennsylvania "Blue Laws," as the restrictive ordinances were called. The nascent NFL had determined that a necessary condition for establishing an NFL franchise was the ability to schedule games on Sunday.

On Saturday, October 21, 1933, several thousand marchers, members of more than one hundred churches in North Philadelphia, launched their march at Frankford and Lehigh Avenues in Kensington. Bearing American flags and banners denouncing the "Open Sunday" proposals, the crowd wended through the streets of Kensington before terminating at McPherson Square. There the marchers were joined by another several thousand protesters and a program of spirited speeches was carried out in which the secularization of Sunday was characterized as a sign of cultural devolution and the rejection of the kind of society that the Founding Fathers had envisioned. The referendum, held on Tuesday, November 11th, did not offer the result the protesters had hoped for. The "Blue Laws" were overturned in a landslide victory for the likes of Bert Bell, who went on to establish the Philadelphia Eagles. Not unrelatedly, the election was also a referendum on prohibition, which had been instituted in 1919 by constitutional amendment. The "wets" scored a decisive victory over the "drys," and the 18th amendment would be repealed one month later on December 5th with the enactment of the 21st amendment.

CHAPTER 6

SOUTH OF THE SQUARE

Lehigh Viaduct, the Visitation. the Bromley Mill, the Thomas A. Edison High School, the 1960 el derailment

Leaving the precincts of MacPherson Square and continuing along Kensington Avenue heading south, one descends toward old Kensington accompanied by a marked change of atmosphere. No longer the commercially vibrant environs of K & A, this segment of the avenue envelops one in a sensorium of gloom and desolation. Prevailing here are assorted cut-rate superettes, check-cashing establishments, dingy taprooms, and pawn shops interspersed among time-worn residences and rows of shuttered store fronts. All of this dreariness sits in the shadow of the el. Foot traffic decreases, and up ahead, just below Somerset Street, the stygian corridor beneath the Lehigh viaduct comes into view. This darkened tunnel under the viaduct, which extends about half the length of a football field, has recently served as a makeshift camp for the homeless. The tunnel is lined with guano-encrusted metal stanchions supporting the crisscrossing trestles of the el and viaduct as well as being enclosed by walls along the sidewalk caked with grime and graffiti. Periodically, Philadelphia's finest has cleared the sidewalks of the improvised encampment. The block serves, along with MacPherson Square, as an index of what Kensington has become.

Rather than taking a stroll under the viaduct, one can opt to turn off onto Tusculum Street which intersects Kensington Avenue just shy of the viaduct. The block of Tusculum Street to the east of the avenue has been immortalized in the 1976 film, *Rocky*. The house of Rocky Balboa, the eponymous protagonist of the epic film, is located on this block. The narrow, time-worn rowhouse served as an apt dwelling for the hard-bitten underdog.

Turning west onto Tusculum Street takes one to the so-called "black bridge," though of late it is painted sometimes white and sometimes blue. The black bridge is located over the old Pennsylvania Railroad tracks—the rail line which cut a swath across North Philadelphia and served the succession of factories straddling Lehigh Avenue.

Crossing the bridge, one was immediately confronted by the magnificently monstrous John Bromley and Sons textile mill. The mill occupied one entire block along Lehigh Avenue bounded by "A" Street on the west and "B" Street on the east. This massive structure closed shop by the 1970s, and subsequently succumbed to a number of fires throughout the 1970s. A single fire was inadequate to dispatch this behemoth. On the night of July 30th, 1979, the conclusive fire broke out, and the next day's edition of the Philadelphia Inquirer features a large, front-page photo showing the interior of the building engulfed in flames behind the five-story façade. The rows of tightly-spaced windows are brightly illuminated by the blaze while a large piece of façade pulls away trailed by a massive tongue of flame.[8] The wrecking ball would later deliver the coup de grace to the charred remnants of the structure. In its place, there now stands a bland welfare office in the middle of a spacious parking lot—a significant architectural downgrade from the awesome Bromley structure.

Historic American Buildings Survey, Creator. John Bromley & Sons Building, 201-263 Lehigh Avenue, Philadelphia, Philadelphia County, PA. Documentation Compiled After. Photograph. Retrieved from the Library of Congress, <www.loc.gov/item/pa0828/>

The spectacular Bromley mill fire was no anomaly. It has been a tragic consequence of deindustrialization that fires have become the bane of the neighborhood. With so many vacant factories, especially on Lehigh Avenue, parallel to the Pennsylvania Railroad tracks, residents in this district of Kensington have grown accustomed to recurrent conflagrations. Therein lies the particularly tragic feature of these terrific blazes. With banks of rowhouses set cheek to jowl with hulking mills, these fires tend to take out dozens of residences, as flying embers fill the air and settle wherever the wind carries them.

The 1994 blaze, which reduced the huge Quaker Lace Company mill at 4th and Lehigh to rubble, wiped out a dozen rowhouses on the 2700 block of Lawrence Street, each catching fire one after the other, "like dominoes," according to one resident quoted in the September 20th edition of the *Philadelphia Inquirer*.[9] Dozens more residents had to evacuate their homes as embers rained down on surrounding streets. Many of the fires, which are steadily reducing the number of Kensington's great monuments to industry, have been triggered by arson. Some of those mills which have escaped immolation at the hands of arsonists have been converted into apartment buildings or upscale condominiums. Others such as the Crane Arts building, a former warehouse located at 1400 North American Street, have been appropriated as artists' studios,.

Fortunately, the Bromley fire in 1979 left the south side of Lehigh Avenue, occupied by the Visitation Church and the Episcopal Hospital across from the mill, relatively unscathed. The avenue is one of the widest thoroughfares in the city. There is something unearthly about this stretch of the avenue. On the twin spires of the Visitation church are highlighted oxidized copper outlines featuring acute angles which appear as if they are about to unfold and materialize into two fabulous birds taking flight. The Visitation Catholic Church is notable on two fronts. First, it has survived the wave of church closures in Kensington that has taken place over the past several decades. Such closures have brought down St. Boniface (demolished), the Ascension, St. Edward the Confessor at 8th and York Streets, and St. Joan of Arc at Frankford Avenue and Atlantic Street (the church currently functions as a satellite church for Holy Innocents church in the nearby neighborhood of Juniata). The history of the church features an eerie incident recounted on the Philadelphia Church Project website.[10] Founded as St. Cecilia's Church in the early 1870s, the church underwent a name change after the current church building was built to replace the smaller, original church. Shortly after the dedication of the new church building in the latter part of the decade, the parish priest there was awakened in the middle of the night by the ringing of the church bells. Fearing that there had been a break-in, the priest apprehensively hurried over to the church. There he discovered two small children praying and weeping before the altar. Being asked what they were doing in the church, the children indicated to the bewildered priest that their father was dying at the neighboring Episcopal Hospital and was facing death without the benefit of the last rites. The priest thereupon hurried over to the hospital and indeed it was as the children had described—a man with the name the children had provided was in his death throes. The man indicated that he was alone in the world, and inquired as to how the priest knew that he was dying in the hospital. The man was astonished to hear the priest describe his own two children. The patient informed the priest that his two children had both died in childhood. The man cried out to the priest, "My two children returned from heaven to ensure that I received the sacrament of Extreme Unction!" The two wraithlike "visitors" facilitated their father's happy death and begot the current designation of the church—the Church of the Visitation. At least that is how the legend characterizes the designation of the church as the Church of the "Visitation." Technically, however, the official name of the church is Church of the Visitation of the Blessed Virgin Mary.

Progress of Steel Construction, Perspective of Kensington Ave. & Lehigh Ave,. looking south, October 23, 1916. (The twin spires of the Church of the Visitation are visible in the center background of the image, and the Bromley and Sons textile mill is visible in the center right.)
Courtesy of the Library Company of Philadelphia

Unstated in the narrative, though perhaps suggested implicitly, is the misfortune of the Catholic man, in his moribund condition, having ended up in a Protestant hospital. The anti-Catholic riots remained fresh in the memory of Kensington residents, having taken place several decades prior, and interreligious tensions remained high. No opportunity was lost to score points against the other side, nor to give vent to stored-up resentments. No worse fate could befall a dying Catholic, so the legend seems to suggest, than to have to breathe one's last in a Protestant hospital.

This circuit through Upper Kensington would not be complete without continuing further west along Lehigh Avenue past the tall and forbidding tower of the Episcopal Hospital and the old Quaker Lace Company mill site, to the location of the first high school in Kensington. Currently, the site at 7th Street and Lehigh features a nondescript strip mall, at the entrance to which, however, stands a historical marker bearing witness to the Thomas A. Edison High School that formally occupied the site and to the "Edison 64." The marker pays tribute to the sixty-four alumni of Edison High School who made the ultimate sacrifice to their country during the Vietnam War.

The first incarnation of Edison High School was as the Northeast Manual Training School, which opened on Girard Avenue at Howard Street in 1890. At that time, secondary school education was just beginning to represent a worthwhile pursuit for the children of working-class families. As the first response to the call for an educational opportunity beyond elementary school, the Northeast Manual Training School was for boys only, and offered primarily vocational training consistent with a neighborhood setting dedicated to industrial production.

In 1905 the Girard Avenue vocational school relocated to new quarters in the Fairhill section of Kensington, on Lehigh Avenue between 7th and 8th Streets, in an architecturally impressive building that featured Gothic towers, gargoyles, and intricate engravings. The dedication ceremony was a grandiose community event at which the president of Princeton University, Woodrow Wilson, delivered the main address. Six years later, the name of the school was changed to Northeast Public High School. Over time, the curriculum broadened and the school earned a reputation for academic excellence. As a widely celebrated scholastic institution, it became a site which merited a place on the celebrity-visitation circuit, and enjoyed visits between the wars by Babe Ruth, Marion Anderson, and Albert Einstein. In 1951, the school was the recipient of the Bellamy Award—a national award given annually to a high school demonstrating outstanding academic achievement. But despite that award, the fortunes of the school had already begun to alter significantly during the 1950s, owing to the deindustrialization of Kensington, the growing racial diversification of the neighborhood, and white flight. In 1953, the Northeast Public Alumni Association began campaigning for a new building for the school, giving as the ostensible rationale for their request the growing decrepitude of the building. Meanwhile, the so-called "Great Northeast" section of Philadelphia was beginning to serve as a popular landing zone for those engaged in "white flight" from Kensington. A new school building was approved to be constructed in the Rhawnhurst neighborhood of the Great Northeast at Cottman and Algon Avenues. Rhawnhurst, like most other sections of the Great Northeast at that time, was uniformly white. But the "new" school that would be created was not the one that would occupy the spanking new building constructed on Cottman Avenue, but the one occupying the old building on Lehigh Avenue, which was re-christened as the Thomas A. Edison Public High School. The entire historical legacy of Northeast Public High School was removed to the new site—the name of the school, all awards and sports trophies, even two stained glass windows honoring Northeast graduates who served in World War I. The "new" school on Lehigh Avenue would begin its new life with an empty trophy case.

The advocates of the move alleged that, whatever the overt rationale, the Great Northeast needed a school and at the same time the Lehigh Avenue facility stood in need of renovation. Added to the list of complaints about the old building was that the athletic facilities were located inconveniently more than a mile away at 25th and Clearfield Streets. All these avowed pretexts skirted what the optics suggested, namely, that the plan was driven by racism. A study conducted in 2001-2002 at the school, as a U. S. history class project,[11] reports that African-American students accounted for 4.7% of the student body in 1947 and 46.4% of the student body in 1957. Meanwhile, the pride which Northeast Public had always felt regarding the numbers of its graduates that performed military service in the country's wars was carried on at the "new" school on Lehigh Avenue (the death toll was 35 graduates of Northeast in World War I and over 300 in World War II). The website of the Vietnam Memorial reports that "Thomas Edison High School in Philadelphia sustained the largest number of Vietnam War casualties of any high school in the nation with 54." A book entitled *Edison 64,* written by Richard Sand and published in 2019, reports the casualties as numbering 64. Whatever the reasons for the discrepancy between the two numbers, the school in fact has earned the somber distinction of having among its alumni the highest number of Vietnam War deaths.[12] Of those 64 graduates of Northeast who lost their lives, 42 were African-American or Latino.[13]

Meanwhile, despite its deteriorating condition, the Lehigh Avenue facility remained occupied as the Thomas Edison High School until 1988 when the school moved into new quarters at Front and Luzerne Streets, a little over a mile to the north in the Feltonville neighborhood. Between 1988 and 2002, the Julia de Burgos Middle School inhabited the venerable Lehigh Avenue building. After 2002 the building sat vacant, progressively deteriorating until a fire gutted the building in August of 2011 and the building succumbed to wrecking ball. The site now features a strip mall. At the entrance to the shopping complex, a historical marker commemorates the Edison 64.

> **THOMAS A. EDISON HIGH SCHOOL AND THE VIETNAM WAR**
>
> Sixty-four former Edison students died in service to their country during the Vietnam War between 1965 and 1971-more than any school in the nation. These young men represent the burden and disparity of the war on poor rural and urban communities throughout America. Whether they enlisted voluntarily or were assigned draft numbers that they were unable to avoid by deferment, these men made the ultimate sacrifice.
>
> PENNSYLVANIA HISTORICAL AND MUSEUM COMMISSION 2014

    Backtracking along Lehigh Avenue heading east, one arrives at Front Street. Turning right on that street in the direction of downtown is one of the main thoroughfares of the Puerto Rican community. Looming ahead is the busy intersection of Front Street, Kensington Avenue, and York Street. Frankford el trains negotiate above this intersection heading south, the sharp turn from Kensington Avenue onto Front Street. The angle is acute enough that the train, having slowed, issues a prolonged, banshee-like squeal throughout the duration of the turn.

    On the evening of December 26th, 1961, a southbound train contrived to derail by failing to slow down sufficiently, the lead car smashing into the guardrail along the crook of the curve. It was propelled by momentum and plowed into the platform of the York-Dauphin el station. "El Jumps Track, One Dead, 35 Hurt," announced the next day's headline of the *Philadelphia Inquirer*.[14] Several photos featured below the news headline show the crumpled lead car tilted to the side and the wrecked interior of the car with a crumpled undercarriage and seats knocked askew. The impact of the crash caused chunks of guardrail and pieces of masonry to rain down on the street below. The passenger who was killed was a 64-year-old man on his way to his job as a night security guard at the Lit Brothers department store. Seated in the lead car, he was crushed against the station platform. The train was one of the sleek, newly-introduced stainless steel trains, which, around 1960, were beginning to replace the old, original trains. The shiny new cars with their bright interiors contrasted sharply with the dark, clunky old coaches, which would rumble along ponderously before coming to a stop at each station with a high pitch squeal. At least one conductor got carried away by the stream-lined sleekness of the new trains. The accident occurred shortly before midnight, and had it taken place during the rush hour, the consequences could have been catastrophic. The trains bore thousands of commuters during rush hour heading to workplaces downtown, and northbound trains bore hundreds of North Catholic High School students heading to the Erie-Torresdale station. The trains carried a significant number of students each day since North Catholic was claimed by some to be, during the 1950s, the largest high school in the world. It was not an implausible claim.

PART II:

LOWER KENSINGTON

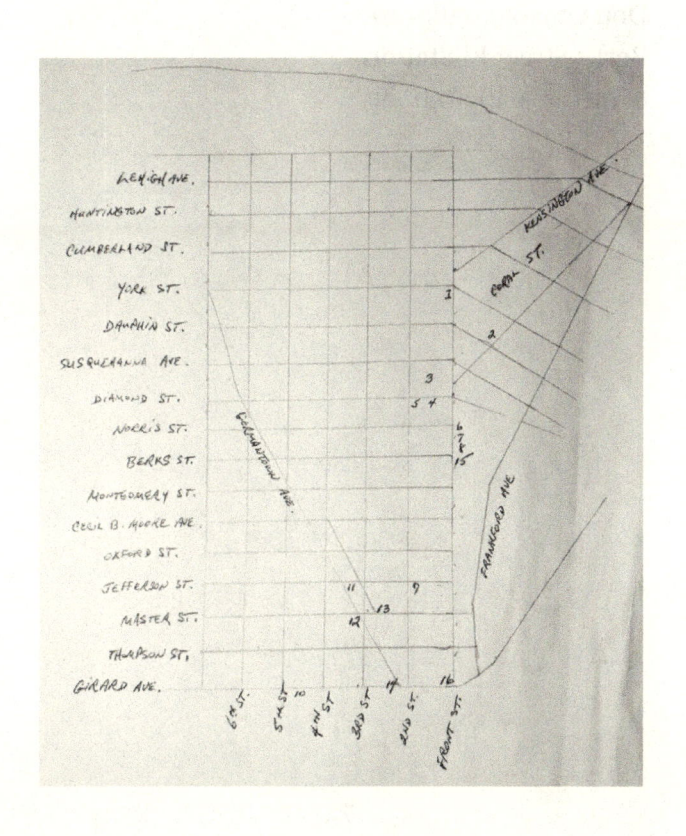

Charles Lutz

1. York-Dauphin El Station
2. Coral Street house where Knights of Labor was founded
3. Norris Square
4. Kensington Hospital
5. St Boniface Church (demolished)
6. Newt's (now the Shissler Recreation Center)
7. Old Kensington Depot (demolished)
8. Kensington Creative and Performing Arts High School
9. St. Michael's Church
10. St Peter's Church
11. Crane Arts building
12. Cohocksink RR Depot (gone)
13. Nanny Goat Market (gone)
14. Don Quixote sculpture
15. Berks Street El Station
16. Girard Ave El Station

CHAPTER 7

NORRIS SQUARE AND ENVIRONS

The Harbison's Milk Bottle, Norris Square

Anyone traversing the length of Kensington, starting from K & A on the way to downtown, even if directionally challenged can do no wrong by keeping the downtown-bound el in view. Where Kensington Avenue terminates at the intersection of Front and York Streets, the walker proceeds south along Front Street. Narrower than Kensington Avenue, Front Street is more swathed in shade owing to the el, and if the train windows were open, it's as if the commuter could reach out and touch the opposing building facades. For the walker, the evidence of post-industrial deterioration along the street is plainly visible in the landscape of shuttered storefronts, vacant lots where deteriorating structures have been demolished, check-cashing venues, cut-rate clothing stores, and the like.

Approaching Susquehanna Avenue, one catches a glimpse of a patch of green to the west of Front Street. Norris Square, bounded by Diamond St and Susquehanna Avenue on the south and north respectively, and by 2nd and Mascher Streets on the west and east, is a small remnant of greenery in what was once a primeval woodland.

The Norris family was one of the original Quaker families

that settled in Philadelphia as William Penn undertook his holy experiment in the 17th century. Isaac Norris had acquired wealth prior to his move to Philadelphia by virtue of business dealings in the West Indies, which included involvement in the slave trade. In 1717 Norris constructed a country mansion to the north of the city on a plot of land measuring almost one and a half square miles known as Fairhill. The city's northern boundary at the time being Vine Street, Fairhill was significantly exurban. Building a country estate was a popular enterprise among the social elite of the time, and Quaker families such as that of Isaac Norris sought to abide by the counsel that William Penn provided in his *Some Fruits of Solitude and Reflection* of 1682: "The country life is to be preferred; for there we see the works of God; but in cities little else but the works of men."[15] Obviously it helps if one has sufficient wealth to build an opulent estate in a pristine refuge, but Fairhill ultimately was not to retain its idyllic character. The tidal wave of industrialization swept away the sylvan retreat in the nineteenth century, leaving in its wake a congested mass of factories and tightly-packed rowhouses. What greenery remained included Norris Square on the eastern edge, and a Quaker cemetery on the western edge of Fairhill where the remains of Lucretia Mott, the noted Quaker, abolitionist, and women's rights activist, are interred.

The Post-Industrial age brought a transformation of Fairhill into what is known as the "Badlands," so-called because this corner of Kensington is regarded as a hotbed of drug-related violence. The Badlands has acquired some notoriety as a singularly dangerous neighborhood, and provided the setting of the 1994 novel, *Third and Indiana*, written by Steve Lopez. Fairhill and the "Badlands" lie on the western periphery of Kensington, and sprawl across both its upper and lower sections. The walker taking the most direct route to downtown from K &

A bypasses the notorious precinct.

Lately, the immediate environs of the square which bears the Isaac Norris name have undergone a facelift brought about largely through the efforts of the local neighborhood association. In the '50s, '60s, and '70s, walkers en route to downtown from Upper Kensington would have noted increasing dilapidation as they descended into Lower Kensington. At one time the area was tagged with the label "needle square" due to its reputation as a popular drug marketplace. Currently, Norris Square is now girded with many spruced-up rowhouses. Some of these dwellings have three stories and many feature brownstone balustrades and worn, but tastefully restored, brick masonry facades. The feeling of urban chic is becoming palpable.

On Diamond Street along the southern edge of Norris Square, two neighborhood fixtures interpose themselves amid rows of residences—the Kensington Hospital and the Saint Boniface Catholic parish compound. The small Kensington Hospital has proven itself to be a resilient holdover when mega-hospitals have been commanding the field in recent decades. The Kensington Hospital for Women started in the 1880s in a rowhouse at 136 Diamond Street. Over time, the facility expanded by acquiring several adjacent rowhouses and established itself as a quality maternity-care center. The hospital closed in 1945, but reopened the following year as a general hospital. Currently, the facility offers detox services and short-term acute care for infectious conditions.

While the Kensington Hospital has survived the vicissitudes of time as a Norris Square landmark, the other noteworthy edifice along Diamond Street has not. The Saint Boniface church stood on the south side of Diamond Street between Hancock and Mascher Streets overlooking Norris Square for more than 100 years. The church was aptly named for Saint Boniface, the 8th century native of Britain who brought Christianity to the Germans. The church was established to serve the ever-increasing numbers of German immigrants settling in Kensington. The other German national parish, Saint Peter's (which was located nine blocks to the south on Girard Avenue), could not accommodate the large number of immigrants. In the decades after the church was dedicated in 1872, a rectory, convent, elementary school, and parish hall were added to the complex, the centerpiece of which remained the brownstone church with its tall spire.

Generations of children were educated in the school, staffed by the Sisters of Notre Dame, and, noting the escalation of educational ambitions during the early decades of the 20th century, the parish inaugurated a post-8th grade commercial school for girls in 1919. By mid-century the mission of serving the German community lost cogency, as neighborhood demographics had shifted. During the decades following World War II, increasing numbers of Latino parishioners prompted the scheduling of liturgical services in Spanish. By the 1970s, the Archdiocese deemed it no longer feasible for parish schools to offer tuition-free education. Enrollment declined, and at the same time the costs of upkeep for the complex of buildings began exceeding the financial means of the parish. The closure of the parish was announced in 2006. Protective scaffolding had to be put in place above the sidewalk before the facade of the church to prevent injury to pedestrians due to falling masonry. The church building along with the convent next to the church on the east were razed in 2012, and 3-story residential units were constructed on the site. Meanwhile, the old rectory building on the corner of Diamond and Hancock Streets has become the headquarters of the Norris Square Community Alliance.

When one continues to head south leaving the precincts of Norris Square, it can be noted that to the east there is a water tower in the shape of a milk bottle poised atop a nineteenth century warehouse. The rusted milk bottle is a vestige of the once thriving creamery—the Harbison's Dairy—which operated a fleet of trucks that delivered bottled milk. The milkman would deposit bottles of milk on the doorsteps of Kensington homes every morning, correspondingly collecting the empties for recycling in an early nod to enlightened environmentalism. The company closed shop in the 1960s and the dairy complex stood vacant for several decades until, in recent years, conversion of the old warehouse into apartments was proposed. The milk bottle was designated as a historical landmark and will apparently remain, presumably in its deoxidized splendor, atop the completed residential structure. Commuters using the Frankford el will still be able to gaze upon the oversized bottle with a feeling of satisfaction and children will experience a feeling of awe over the perceived voluminous amount of milk contained therein. (During 2020 the expected facelift of the supersized milk bottle was completed.)

CHAPTER 8

"NEWT'S" AND THE KENSINGTON DEPOT

The east side of Front Street, just south of the whimsical milk bottle, was occupied for many decades during the second half of the twentieth century by a ball field surfaced with black cinders. The cinder playing field at Newt's, as the playground was colloquially referred to, was not unique in Kensington. Generations of kids reared in Kensington during the twentieth century were accustomed to conducting athletic competitions on hard concrete, either in local schoolyards or on black cinder fields. The Hissey playground in Upper Kensington at "C" Street and Indiana Avenue also sported a field covered in black cinders. Generally speaking, the color green was never very evident in Kensington, as the neighborhood is historically photosynthesis-deprived. At any rate, the absence of flora obviated the need for much maintenance such as mowing. If pieces of black cinder often featured sharp edges, it goes without saying that long pants were a wise choice if one was anticipating a hard slide into home plate during a baseball game.

Newt's stood on a multi-acre plot that began its existence as the terminus of the Philadelphia and Trenton rail line which was established in the 1830s. The line was one of the earliest rail lines in an ever-expanding network of railways that took off in the

1830s and 1840s. The network served the burgeoning industrial sector in Kensington as well as the travel needs of the general population. The line was barely inaugurated when it was determined that the Kensington Depot at Berks Street by Front would not quite do—it was deemed necessary to extend the line further south into downtown Philadelphia. When construction began in 1839 on the project to lay track down the middle of Front Street in the direction of Girard Avenue, residents along and around that stretch of Front Street were roused into action. Whatever construction teams laboriously accomplished during the day was promptly undone by housewives and their husbands and children at night. Railroad ties set into the street were dislodged and clefts in the roadway left by dislodged crossties were filled. Construction crews were frequently harassed and were driven off on more than one occasion. The determination of the residents is understandable—few would relish a noisy, multi-ton, block of ferrous metal spouting a shower of sparks while chugging back and forth before one's residence numerous times a day. Kenneth Milano in his book, *The Philadelphia Nativist Riots*, provides a brief sketch of the "Railroad Riots" of 1840-1842 in Kensington as a kind of prelude to the more sanguinary riots in Kensington in 1844.[16] The railroad company ultimately threw in the towel, but the Kensington Depot and Freight Station would continue in use during the 19th century.

During the 20th century the depot would fall into disuse and the Pennsylvania Railroad would devise a new routing for its line farther north along the top of Upper Kensington that would cross Broad Street and the Schuylkill River into the western edge of downtown Philadelphia. In the early twentieth century, Front Street would serve as one of the arteries hosting the Frankford El. Of course, the trains of the el were electric, and the rails were elevated above the street.

In 2010-2011 there were changes that transformed the old Kensington Depot site. First of all, green grass replaced the black cinders of Newt's, which had been rechristened as the Shissler Recreation Center. A new public high school opened on the southern edge of the field—the Kensington Creative and Performing Arts High School. This school of approximately five hundred students is an index, like nothing else, of a new Kensington. The school is proudly described as the first LEED Platinum certified school building in the United States. LEED represents a green building certification program. Besides that distinguishing feature, the student body features a significant amount of racial and ethnic heterogeneity. The school is coed, which is a significant break with tradition as generations of high school students in Kensington attended single-sex high schools. The academic program is weighted towards the arts, indicative of a new trend in Lower Kensington whereby the formerly industrial district is now on the cusp of becoming a haven for artists.

Nearby, at 1400 North American Street, the handsomely rehabbed Crane Arts Building, offers art studios and exhibition space in what was formerly a warehouse constructed in 1905. At 1417 North 2nd Street, the Pig Iron Theatre Company occupies the old Saint Michael's Elementary School. The performing arts program was inaugurated in 1995.

CHAPTER 9

NATIVISM AND THE 1844 NATIVIST RIOTS

Upon moving on from the old Kensington Depot hard by the Berks Street El Station, one draws near to the site of one of the most tragic events in the history of Kensington. The Nativist riots of July 1844 left dozens dead, several blocks of homes set ablaze, and St Michael's church at 2nd and Masters St reduced to ashes. The riots occurred due to a variety of factors, chief among which was the enmity between Irish Catholic immigrants, most of whom arrived in Kensington in the 1830s and 1840s, and the Protestant Scotch-Irish immigrants who arrived earlier during the second half of the 18th century. The rioting, sometimes referred to as the Kensington Bible Riots, represents a significant chapter in the history of immigration in the United States. The enmity between native-born Kensington residents and the newly-arrived Irish Catholics was rooted in the two centuries of religious conflict that unfolded in the British Isles in the 17th and 18th centuries once relations with the Papacy were severed by the English Crown in the 16th century. Reaching back into those centuries sheds light upon the causes of the violence that took place in Kensington in 1844.

The British North American colonies played a role in the ongoing religious conflicts in the British Isles insofar as they served as an attractive refuge for religious dissidents who had grown tired of a religious climate in which the Church of England had become the privileged, State-sanctioned church. Religious dissidents at the time largely included those sects seeking the elimination of Catholic elements from Christian practice. For them, the Church of England, as the so-called *via media* representing a compromise between Catholicism and such sects as the Quakers and Puritans, was too Catholic. It goes without saying that such political concepts as American-style separation of Church and State and church affiliation being a matter of free choice were still in a nascent state and would not see the light of day until the end of the 18th century. Failure to sign on to the Church of England at the time subjected one to a variety of penalties which included such measures as denial of access to civil and military positions, denial of access to higher education, or to the possession of firearms, among other restrictions. The notorious Penal Laws were more draconian as applied to Catholics, who were subject to the confiscation of their property.

While a Puritan community was famously established in Massachusetts during the first half of the 17th century, William Penn led a band of Quakers to his land grant of Pennsylvania. Both ventures represented efforts by these religious visionaries to establish their ideal Christian communities in a world unburdened by history. If they viewed the New World as virgin territory, they were not always prepared to acknowledge the rights of the original inhabitants. Penn, for his part however, negotiated a treaty with the Lenape, and an idealized depiction of the ceremonial event painted by Benjamin West hangs in the Pennsylvania Academy of Fine Arts. Whether the Lenape shared the Europeans' understanding of land as a marketable commodity is open to speculation.

Penn also departed from the religious policies which

characterized the Puritan settlement in Massachusetts, insofar as his "holy experiment" included a tolerance for all denominations, at least in theory. Over time, Quaker meeting houses in Philadelphia would share Penn's green country town with other church communities such as the Presbyterians and Anglicans. Even a Catholic church—St. Joseph's—was established in 1733 in Philadelphia, tucked away as inconspicuously as possible in a small courtyard off Willings Alley, and the small Catholic community would be able to conduct its liturgical activities in spite of the English Penal Laws, which technically forbade the celebration of Catholic Mass.

Philadelphia's working-class suburb of Kensington began taking shape as a result of emigration from Ireland. First came the Scotch-Irish in the 18th century—largely Presbyterian by religious affiliation—who had emigrated from Scotland to Ireland (more specifically from the Scottish lowlands to Ulster in northern Ireland). Many were weavers by trade, and they set in motion the textile industry which was to become the premier brand of the manufacturing industry in Kensington.

Later the Irish Catholics arrived, decidedly less moneyed and less skilled than their Scotch-Irish counterparts. Both groups had suffered significant persecution as the result of determined efforts by successive English political regimes to consolidate control over Ireland over the course of several centuries, particularly during the years of the English Civil Wars of the 17th century. When the Commonwealth of England was established in 1649 following the execution of Charles I, Oliver Cromwell led a devastating military campaign against a confederation of Royalist groups in Ireland and crushed the power of those groups, the Catholics being prominent among them, in Ireland. Those Irish who persisted in their allegiance to the Catholic Church suffered severe persecution, such as having their property confiscated. It might be said that the tensions and mutual rancor between the Scotch-Irish Protestants and the Catholic Irish which characterized centuries of Irish history were reproduced transatlantically in Kensington during the early 19th century.

The arrival of the Scotch-Irish immigrants into Kensington pre-dated that of the Irish Catholics. Their emigration from Ireland followed as a consequence to several failed rebellions which broke out in the 18th century in Ireland against the Anglo-Irish establishment, such as the Rebellion of 1798. Many of these emigres were skilled weavers, and thus was launched the textile industry in various locations on the East Coast such as that in Kensington. Kensington was, for the most part, uniformly Protestant when large numbers of Irish Catholics started arriving in the 1830s and 1840s. When those new Catholic immigrants started arriving, many of the Scotch-Irish were second generation, and such native-born status inclined many to regard themselves as the authentic Americans. The religious landscape of the United States as a whole was largely Protestant. The influx of Catholics represented a demographic change threatening to disturb the religious landscape. For many of the native-born class, Protestantism constituted a requisite feature of authentic American identity, along with whiteness, as blacks (despite their being native to the land for generations), were barred from citizenship until the passage of the 14th amendment to the Constitution in 1868.

As far as religion was concerned, it might be added that such Nativist chauvinism tended not to exclude those known as "Deists." Deism was a religion, or more precisely, a philosophical orientation. It was unaffiliated with any organized Christian church, which characterized the outlook of the majority of the educated elite, and of the so-called "founding fathers," for the most part. The Deists affirmed the existence of a creator God, who, upon creating the material world, receded into the background and left the conduct of worldly affairs to human beings. The Deists invested no credence in the central theological doctrines of Christianity, such as the divinity of Christ, the Trinity, the miraculous events narrated in the Gospels, or the existence of a supernatural realm. In other words, they were profound reductionists when it came to theology, but occupied themselves avidly with forging a modern state established on the basis of Enlightenment ideals, such as representative government, separation of Church and State, and guaranteed individual freedoms such as freedom of the press, freedom of speech, freedom to assemble, and so on. At the same time, however, they were disinclined to discredit Christianity openly, because they considered that the Christian religion, at least in its Protestant manifestation, served a useful purpose in instilling morality in the lives of the general citizenry. In their calculation, any weakening of this moral breakwater risked opening the floodgates of immorality in the general population. Needless to say, the Christianity represented in its Catholic expression was not looked upon with favor by the Deists, as the Catholic Church had always stood as a fierce opponent of the Enlightenment and had tended to align itself with what are usually regarded as reactionary political regimes.

The growing numbers of Irish Catholic immigrants in Kensington began getting the attention of native-born Americans during the decade of the 1820s. The efforts to sound the alarm about the threat posed by this new population of immigrants have been characterized as the "Protestant Crusade." Obviously, economics played a role in this growing fear, as these new immigrants were generally very poor and were willing to sell their labor below scale. The Protestant clerical establishment, for its part, grew fearful that these growing numbers of Catholic immigrants were threatening to engulf the religious landscape, ultimately transforming what had been a Protestant majority into a minority.

The case against the Catholic Church was laid out in no uncertain terms in the various media outlets of the time. R.A. Billington published *The Protestant Crusade* in 1938 and lists no less than forty-five newspapers—dailies, weeklies, and monthlies—which appeared in the 1830's and 1840s, the *raison d'etre* of all these being to educate the American public about the theological errors of the Catholic Church and the dire threat posed by the Church to American civic institutions.

It was not only journalism that was active in stoking nativist paranoia, but also book-length narratives appeared which laid out graphically the salacious practices brought to American shores by the influx of Catholic immigrants. The public could indulge their taste for prurient potboilers by reading such works as *Awful Disclosures of the Hotel Dieu Nunnery of Montreal*, written, purportedly, by Maria Monk. The best known of the popular genre which might be termed the "escaped nun" narrative, the account provided the lurid details of life in a nunnery. Maria Monk claimed to have witnessed scenes of what essentially constituted sex slavery in a convent in Montreal—a convent adorned with all the Gothic machinery that characterized the Gothic tale. These included subterranean chambers, secret tunnels, trap doors, and mildewed crypts. Priests satisfied their lust by sneaking into this ghoulish setting via those secret tunnels. Within this dark medieval setting, captive young women were forced to submit to sexual abuse and sadistic practices, and whatever babies resulted from the various kinds of perversion inflicted upon these women were summarily strangled upon being baptized, and cast into a deep pit where they were covered in lime. Such narratives aroused sufficient outrage that calling for investigations of nunneries became a *de rigeur* feature of Know Nothing political platforms. No evidence was ever uncovered that gave foundation to any of the claims made by Maria Monk, who was eventually exposed as a fraud and her book a sham. The recent study, *Escaped Nuns: True Womenhood and the Campaign against Convents in Antebellum America,* by Cassandra Yacovazzi, lays out the historical details of this episode.

Were these objections to Catholicism purely a reflection of paranoia, ignorance, and simple animus toward whomever practices the Christian faith differently? Well, not entirely. The Catholic Church never jumped on the Enlightenment bandwagon and the French Revolution amply confirmed to the Church hierarchy that these modern Enlightenment ideas portended a devolution towards cultural collapse. Those Enlightenment notions such as constitutional government, separation of Church and State, the notion that only through human reason can truth be apprehended, among others, are tenets against which the Church fought fiercely up until the 2nd Vatican Council held in the early 1960s. It was only at that ecumenical council, summoned by Pope John XXIII, when the magisterium of the Church, after intense debate, gave endorsement to democracy, freedom of religion, and representative government—the hallmarks of the American political system.

Furthermore, at the time when the so-called Protestant Crusade was underway in the United States, the Pope was still a political leader—in fact, an autocrat—as well as the spiritual head of the Catholic Church. The country over which the Pope ruled—the Papal States—stretched from coast-to-coast in the middle of the Italian peninsula, with Rome as its capital. The Pope governed the territory as a theocratic state, and as its autocratic ruler. But during the decades that spanned the middle of the 19th century, trouble was brewing for the Pope and his domains.

The Napoleonic era was followed by an extended period of nationalism and political liberalism throughout Europe, which included an independence movement for an Italian national state. The Popes, as emblems of despotism, stood as obstacles to the democratic aspirations of the Italian freedom-fighters. But in 1846, Pius IX assumed the papacy, successor to the arch-conservative Gregory XVI. Known as a progressive, the newly-elected Pius IX gave heart to European liberals. And indeed Pius IX wasted no time in enacting a series of liberal reforms. Among these reforms were the easing of restrictions on the press, granting amnesty to political dissidents, bringing laypersons into the employ of the Vatican, and lifting restrictions on Jews by allowing them to leave the Jewish ghetto. But when the revolutions of 1848 swept across Europe, among the objectives of which was the creation of a unified Italian state into which the Papal States would be absorbed, the Pope began reassessing where he stood politically. Disinclined to accede to the absorption of his Papal States into a free, unified Italy, which would end the Pope's days as a temporal ruler, the Pope jumped off the liberal bandwagon. When a Roman Republic was declared following military successes scored by Italian independence fighters, the Pope was forced into exile. The French army, a year later, dislodged the revolutionaries from Rome and restored the Papal States with Pius IX as its sovereign. The experience converted Pius IX unto a hardline conservative.

The anti-democratic nature of Papal governance in the Papal States as well as the Church's pronouncements unfriendly to democratic institutions, played a significant role in fueling anti-Catholic fears in the wake of Irish-Catholic immigration to the United States. Whether or not these poor, largely uneducated Irish immigrants really thought about or cared much about the far-away pontiff is open to speculation. At any rate anti-Catholic societies were founded, such as the American Protestant Society, whose constitution, published in *The American Protestant Vindicator*, in 1840, proclaimed: "the principles of the court of Rome are totally irreconcilable with the gospel of Christ, liberty of conscience, the rights of man, and with the constitution and laws of the United States of America . . . We believe the system of Popery to be, in its principles and tendency, subversive of civil and religious liberty, and destructive to the spiritual welfare of men."[17]

Throughout the 1840s and into the 1850s, a robust populist movement driven by anti-immigrant sentiment gathered steam, characterized by the phenomenon of what is known as Know-Nothingism. That expression was coined by the journalist Horace Greeley to describe those secretive societies, such as the Order of the Star-Spangled Banner, which strove to suppress voting rights of immigrants and place restrictions on their path to citizenship. Once feeling sufficient confidence in their political clout, Know-Nothing groups consolidated themselves into a political party in the 1850s called the American Party. The party scored a number of congressional victories in the 1850s, and during the 1856 presidential campaign year they fielded Millard Fillmore as a candidate for president. In 1848 Fillmore had become Vice-President to Zachery Taylor, comprising the Whig ticket, and he assumed the presidency when Taylor died in 1850. Fillmore failed to obtain his party's nomination for president in 1852, and he returned to private life. Fillmore was summoned out of retirement by the American Party in 1856, and as the American Party's candidate in the 1856 election, Fillmore received 21% of the popular vote, losing to Democrat James

Buchanan. During the final years of the 1850s, tensions over the issue of slavery were boiling over and anxieties related to the influx of Catholic immigrants from Ireland and Germany took second place to the sectional division over the issue of slavery.

Paranoia features prominently in any eruption of nativism in American history. The political activities of that brand of Nativism known as the Know-Nothing movement were driven by a conspiracy theory, the central thrust of which was that these recent Catholic arrivals from Europe represented an advance guard which would open the way for a Papal takeover of the nation. The American Party—the chief political arm of the Know-Nothings—sounded that drumbeat throughout much of the decade of the 1850s. But the typical immigrant family, largely without advanced education and driven by economic concerns, was consumed with earning a living, often tenuously, and rearing children. As much as the far-away Church hierarchy may have endorsed regressive stateship in its edicts, poor immigrants such as those who settled in Kensington were the unlikeliest of effective agents of an insidious, subversive design.

It was not only the perceived anti-democratic authoritarianism of the Catholic Church which disturbed the non-Catholic population, but Catholic theology also came under attack. The Church was seen as being loaded down with theological accretions that had no foundation in Sacred Scripture, accretions largely dating from the Middle Ages. The Protestant clerical establishment was determined to leave no doubt that Catholic theology was at odds with authentic Christianity. The catalogue of Catholic theological errors generally included such practices as the veneration of Mary and the saints, the doctrine of purgatory, the practice of granting indulgences, the Papacy, the doctrine of transubstantiation, among many others. But how these so-called "errors" were understood was usually not congruent with the exact theological significance of these practices in the Church. For example, the term "transubstantiation" is indeed a term introduced by Thomas Aquinas in the 13th century, during the time when Aristotelian philosophy had become the fashion. The term was intended to offer an explanation of the doctrine of the Real Presence, that is, the belief that the words of consecration during the Mass transform the bread and wine into the body and blood of Jesus Christ. That is to say, the theological doctrine in question is that of the Real Presence—the term "transubstantiation" was, and is, intended simply to provide one approach to understanding the meaning of the doctrine. Aquinas, by utilizing the categories of Aristotelian philosophy to facilitate an understanding of the Real Presence, was doing what theologians always do, namely, using contemporary language in order to elucidate a theological doctrine. John the Evangelist did the same thing in the 4th Gospel, using concepts drawn from Platonic philosophy, such as "logos," in order to characterize who Christ is. The notion of transubstantiation does not add new doctrine; it was simply intended to clarify what was already taught and believed. The typical Catholic believer—then and now—may have no idea what the term transubstantiation means, but any practicing Catholic is familiar with the meaning of the Real Presence. The original Christian communities were certainly zealous in retaining their devotion to the Real Presence in the Eucharist. In fact, it was belief in the Real Presence which contributed to the formal definition of Christ's divine nature during the debates which took place during the period of the Arian controversy.

Arianism, during the first several centuries of Christianity, denied that Christ is God and insisted that he is a creature, subordinate to and not of "one substance" with the Father, created by God, even if he is honored as a kind of demigod. In the face of this Arian theology, many Christian communities began raising the question: *If Christ is not God but was created like any other human being, then what are we receiving when we receive the Eucharist at Mass?* Not all of these early Christians were inclined to engage in formal theological speculation, but when they celebrated the sacrifice of the Mass and received the consecrated bread and wine, they believed that they were communing with God in the flesh, that is, feeding on the very "substance" of God—an example, perhaps, of the theological principle of *lex orandi, lex credendi* at work. That is to say, Christian practice was not something that took shape in the wake of theological formulation, but theological doctrine was formulated as a consequence to theological reflection upon what was already part of religious practice. In that sense, the belief of early Christian communities that they participate in divine life through the reception of the Eucharist rested upon their already established conviction that Christ is God.[18]

Among all these factors contributing to the virulent climate which led to such events as those which took place in Kensington in 1844, a further phenomenon appeared—the Catholic-Protestant debate, arguably the most famous of which was that between the pugnacious John Hughes, the Catholic curate serving in Philadelphia who would later become bishop of New York City, and a Presbyterian clergyman in Philadelphia named John Breckinridge. The two were a study in contrasts. If authentic American-ness was embodied in the native-born Anglo-Protestant population, then John Breckinridge fit the mold. Reared in a family of means, Breckinridge was blessed with impressive patrician credentials. His father was educated at Princeton University. He had been a United States senator from Kentucky and served as Attorney General in Jefferson's cabinet.

Upon completing his studies for the Presbyterian ministry, Breckinridge obtained a ministerial position in Philadelphia in the early 1830s.

For his part, Hughes was an immigrant from Ireland, having grown up in modest circumstances in Ulster where Catholics were subject to significant repression and persecution. Opportunities were rather limited in Ulster for a young Catholic man whose father was a tenant farmer, so at the age of twenty in 1817, Hughes and several other family members immigrated to the United States. He found work as a farm worker and day laborer in Maryland and Pennsylvania. In 1819 he obtained a job as a manual laborer for a community of nuns in Emmitsburg, MD, northeast of Baltimore. This community was founded by Elizabeth Ann Seton, who became the first native-born American saint. Seton saw potential in Hughes for something more than gardening and overseeing the community's slaves. She recommended him for admission into the nearby Mt. Saint Mary's College, where he would ultimately be placed on track for the priesthood. There he would be able to supplement his acerbic temperament with some advanced education in philosophy and theology.

The feud between Hughes and Breckinridge started in the context of a cholera epidemic which afflicted Philadelphia in the early 1830s as outlined in the Richard Shaw biography of Hughes entitled *Dagger John*. The epidemic turned out to be identified as Asiatic cholera, as it was thought to have moved across the globe from Asia, traveling west. As such, nativists were quick to advance the charge that immigrants from Ireland had brought the cholera to American shores. Philadelphia was hit hard by the epidemic in the early years of the 1830s, and as the fatality rate climbed during the summer months of 1831, many Philadelphia residents of sufficient means fled the city to less crowded and less insalubrious environs. The Sisters of Charity from Emmitsburg, MD, notably, were quick to move in the opposite direction, that is, into Philadelphia, in order to minister to the sick and dying. Catholic priests, notably as well, tended to remain at their posts in the city in order to administer the last rites to the dying. Hughes took a jab in print, in the local press, at those Protestant ministers who joined the exodus out of the city. One editor of a nativist newspaper minimized the supposed heroic sacrifice of the Catholic clergy by pointing out that as celibates, they had no families of their own to whom they could carry the infection.[19] That likely represents the sole instance in history of a non-Catholic issuing what in effect is a reasonable justification for the practice of priestly celibacy.

At any rate, eventually an ongoing correspondence between Hughes and Breckinridge was launched which consisted of an exchange of letters in which each argued for their respective claims regarding which church represented the "true church" founded by Christ. Breckinridge rolled out the familiar themes such as that the Catholic Church was opposed to democratic institutions, that the Church rejected the authority of the Bible, that Catholic religious practices were largely unbiblical, and so on. For his part, Hughes, born and reared in Ireland, drew on his childhood experiences in which Catholics were subjected to the British Penal Laws, enforced in the British Isles by Protestant authorities. In one of his letters in 1835, Breckinridge threw down the gauntlet for a face-to-face public debate. Hughes at first declined but eventually agreed to take up the challenge, proceeding with the contest with Breckinridge in spite of his bishop's lack of enthusiasm for what promised to be an acrimonious dogfight. The irenic bishop of Philadelphia, Francis Kendrick, saw little spiritual benefit accruing from such an event, and he discouraged the Catholic faithful from attending the spectacle. A stenographer being employed to make a record of the debate, a transcript of the exchanges between the two contestants was published in 1855.[20] It should be noted that the two contestants allowed for each to make revisions to the transcription, and the stenographer was not always present for the debates.

The published text of the exchanges shows Breckinridge hammering away at the repressive and tyrannical regimes of Catholic countries in Europe, such as Spain, the Hapsburg dominions in central Europe, Rome, and the various states on the Italian peninsula—lands with predominantly Catholic populations where the freedoms which Americans cherish are denied. The implications were obvious—the foreign-born Hughes, being a transplant from Europe, could not be in sympathy with American values. But Hughes did not come from Spain or any other Catholic state where a despotic government, in partnership with the Catholic hierarchy, withheld civil liberties from its populace. Hughes hailed from Ireland, where Catholics languished under the oppressive policies represented in the infamous Penal Laws, imposed by Protestant authorities with the objective of barring Catholics from voting or holding political office, from inheriting property, from possessing firearms, serving in the military, and from obtaining a higher education. Hughes made it clear that he immigrated to America in order to "breathe the air of freedom," because, he emphasized: "I was born under the scourge of Protestant persecution."[21]

Neither Breckinridge nor Hughes held back when it came to *ad hominem* attacks. Fumed Breckinridge: "Nothing could induce me to subject my feelings to the coarse and ill-bred impertinence of a priesthood whose temper and treatment toward other men alternate between servility to their spiritual sovereigns and oppression of their unhappy subjects."[22] Hughes countered with rejoinders such as: "Nothing is more disagreeable than to be obliged to argue with a man who trifles with those rules of reasoning, in the observance of which, the soundness of an argument depends."[23] Hughes took umbrage at the labelling employed by Breckinridge: "'Papist', 'Jesuit', 'native of Ireland', 'foreigner', and every epithet that can awaken a dormant prejudice, or excite a feeling of hatred, is employed to designate the individual whom he himself selected, as his equal in every moral quality."[24] Breckinridge enumerated a litany of suspect practices and teachings associated with the Catholic Church (auricular confession, transubstantiation, Mariolatry, depreciating the Bible, and so on). Hughes targeted the Calvinist doctrine of predestination: "Any doctrine which destroyed free-will and transferred the responsibility of moral transgression from the creature to the Creator, whether true or false in itself, is opposed in its consequences, not only to morality, but to the foundation of all moral laws. But does the Presbyterian doctrine warrant such a conclusion? It certainly does. It teaches that God 'foreordained whatsoever comes to pass.'"[25]

All these aforesaid developments set the stage for dire consequences when Francis Kendrick, bishop of Philadelphia, sent a letter to the Philadelphia school board requesting that Catholic school children be excused from the Bible-reading classes which customarily began the school day in the public schools in Kensington and across the nation (or at least that Catholic school children be permitted to use the Douay-Rheims Bible—the authorized Catholic Bible). Bible study was conducted using the King James version of the Bible, and as long as the student body was homogeneously Protestant, there was no controversy about religion being included in the public education curriculum. Purportedly, Bible readings conducted in class were accompanied by the singing of Protestant hymns as well as by commentary not always friendly to Catholic belief and practice. No doubt parents of Catholic schoolchildren were finding themselves having to field such questions from their children as: *What does it mean to say that the Pope is the anti-Christ? Do we Catholics reject the authority of the Bible? Do Catholics worship Mary and the saints? Is the Catholic Church opposed to democracy and bent upon destroying the freedoms enjoyed in America?* Such reports certainly found their way to the Catholic hierarchy.

The inevitable firestorm was quick to follow. It was predictably charged that the Catholic Church rejects the Bible and is determined to eliminate the Bible from public school education. The school board apparently stalled on Kendrick's request. Thus did an alderman named Hugh Clark—a Catholic and resident of Kensington—march into his neighborhood public school classroom early one morning as Bible reading was being conducted. Confronting the teacher, he snatched the Bible from her hands and tore the book apart. At least one version of the incident offers this account.[26] That the incident produced shock and outrage is to be expected, but presumably, from Clark's perspective, the book was an unauthorized version, and hence invalid.

The local Protestant community now had their *casus belli* and were determined to take to the streets. Leading the charge was one Lewis Levin. Levin had gained a reputation as an anti-Catholic firebrand through his diatribes that had been appearing in several nativist periodicals, such as *The Native American* and *The Daily Sun*. Outdoor oratory being a popular diversion at the time, Levin arranged for a rally to be held in the heart of the Irish-Catholic neighborhood in Kensington, hard by Saint Michael's Catholic Church on 2nd and Master Streets. Apparently for the hot-headed Levin and his nativist devotees, there was no point in staging an anti-immigrant rally unless it was delivered squarely in the maw of the Irish-Catholic population. A makeshift rostrum was set up on an empty lot near the church, and, in a gesture of admirable patriotism, a large American flag was hoisted over the platform. On a warm afternoon of May 3rd, 1844, Levin launched into his vitriol-laden discourse, with several hundred like-minded, immigrant-baiting adherents in the crowd. Catcalls and hooting emanating from Irish-Catholic passersby were followed by rock-throwing, causing Levin and his retinue to beat an inglorious retreat.

But Levin was not someone to bear such ignominy with fainthearted insouciance. Determined to return with more muscle, he arranged for an announcement for a new rally to be prominently placed in *The Native Ame*rican. (For clarification purposes—at the time, the phrase "native American" referred to someone who was native-born, not to an indigenous American.) Infuriated that their rally had been disrupted, the Nativists were determined to vaunt their defiance at the May 6th rally, consequent to "this outrage of a vindictive anti-republic spirit, manifested by a portion of the alien population of Third Ward Kensington."[27]

This time the Nativist rally, held at the same location at 2nd and Master Streets and displaying the *de rigeur* American flag, drew a crowd of over 3,000 nativist sympathizers. The predictable name-calling and rock-throwing ensued until a sudden rainstorm drove the crowd to seek shelter at the nearby block-long covered market called Nanny Goat market. The large American flag that had flown over the rostrum having been secured by the Nativists, the crowd surged towards the market. Suddenly shots rang out, and among those struck by the salvo was a 20-year old nativist sympathizer named George Shifler. Dying within minutes, he was soon declared a nativist martyr.

The shots were presumed to have emanated from the Hibernia Hose Company which was located near the corner of Master and Cadwallader Streets across from the entrance to the market. It was manned by Irish Catholic firefighters who enjoyed a well-earned reputation for rowdyism. A story quickly circulated that amid the turmoil, Shifler had carefully rescued the large American flag from over the speaker's rostrum, evidently to prevent any disrespect to the flag that might be perpetrated by Papist thugs. Images of a mortally-wounded Shifler clutching the rescued flag circulated widely, and a popular ballad was composed celebrating the patriotism of the young hero. The Nativist martyr Shifler was "slain by a ruthless Foreign Band," announces the ballad. It appropriates to itself the virtue of patriotism manifested in its love for the flag: "Our flag's insulted, friends are slain,/And must we quiet be?/No! no! we'll rally round the Flag,/Which leads to victory."

Courtesy of the Library Company of Philadelphia

Charles Lutz

Johnson, Song Publisher, Stationer & Printer, No. 7 N. Tenth St., 3 doors above Market, Phila.

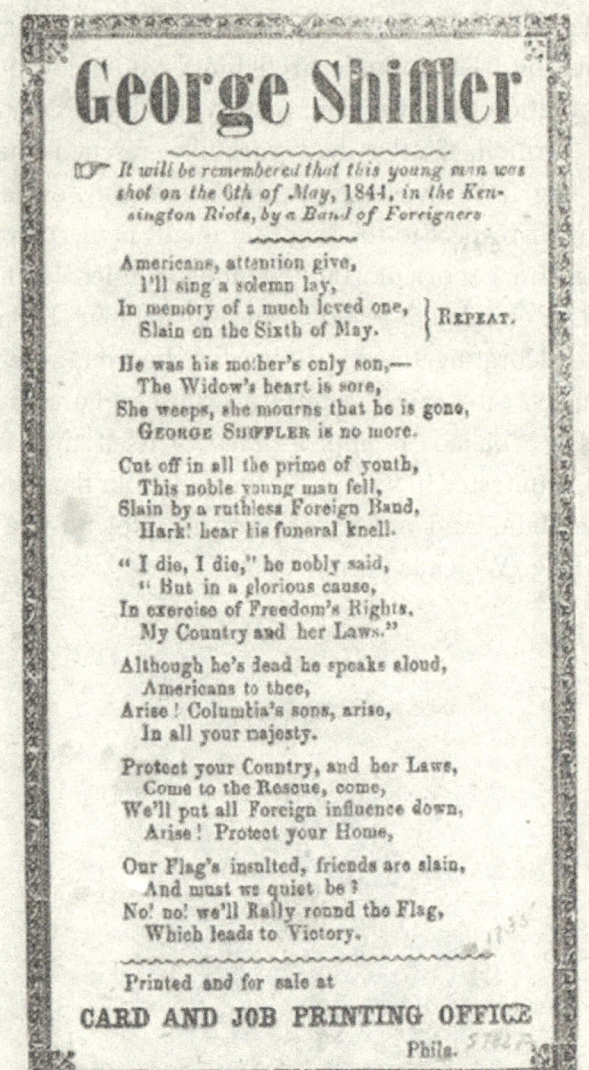

George Shiffler

☞ *It will be remembered that this young man was shot on the 6th of May, 1844, in the Kensington Riots, by a Band of Foreigners*

Americans, attention give,
   I'll sing a solemn lay,
In memory of a much loved one, } REPEAT.
   Slain on the Sixth of May.

He was his mother's only son,—
   The Widow's heart is sore,
She weeps, she mourns that he is gone,
   GEORGE SHIFFLER is no more.

Cut off in all the prime of youth,
   This noble young man fell,
Slain by a ruthless Foreign Band,
   Hark! hear his funeral knell.

"I die, I die," he nobly said,
   "But in a glorious cause,
In exercise of Freedom's Rights,
   My Country and her Laws."

Although he's dead he speaks aloud,
   Americans to thee,
Arise! Columbia's sons, arise,
   In all your majesty.

Protect your Country, and her Laws,
   Come to the Rescue, come,
We'll put all Foreign influence down,
   Arise! Protect your Home,

Our Flag's insulted, friends are slain,
   And must we quiet be?
No! no! we'll Rally round the Flag,
   Which leads to Victory.

Printed and for sale at
CARD AND JOB PRINTING OFFICE
Phila.

Cards, Circulars, Bill-Heads, Hand-Bills, Posters, Labels, Ball, Raffle, Excursion and Party Tickets, Programmes, Ladies' Invitations, Checks, &c., neatly Printed, with accuracy and despatch.

Courtesy of the Library Company of Philadelphia

It deserves mention that it has been a central feature of nativist discourse to incorporate the love of the American flag as an index of patriotism. No one denies that the flag deserves respect, but is patriotism simply a matter of waving the flag, minus any other behavior indicative of love of country? Many of these "Romish foreigners" would go on to give their lives in the upcoming Civil War in defense of the Union, just as immigrants would die in significant numbers in all subsequent American wars. The famous 69th Pennsylvania Infantry Regiment, filled largely by recruits from Philadelphia Irish militia companies, distinguished itself in many of the major battles of the Civil War, including the battle of Gettysburg, during which it suffered hundreds of casualties. It is well-known that minorities, particularly Latinos, were disproportionately represented in the American military during the Vietnam War, while those from wealthier circumstances used their influence to avoid the draft, such as claiming a spurious or less than consequential medical condition. The names of thousands of Latinos are inscribed on the Vietnam Memorial in Washington, and it can be argued that their patriotism is equal to or greater than those who, having grown up in affluence, used their connections to evade military service. Wanting to avoid engagement in a life-threatening activity such as military combat is not something difficult to understand, but if one wants to lay claim to being patriotic, something more must be demanded than simply waving the flag. The spectacle of the draft dodger trumpeting their patriotism by waving the flag—representing a claim to patriotism which is lame, to say the least—can serve as a powerful emetic.

At any rate, the events which took place in Kensington on May 3rd were splashed all over the front pages of the nativist press. On the several days following the incident, rallies were held hard by Independence Hall on Chestnut Street. On May 7th, the crowd was numbered to be in excess of 5,000, all having gathered to obtain an earful, presumably, of nativist rant. The crowd having been worked up to a fever pitch by a series of immigrant-bashing speakers, the chant, "On to Kensington!" started ringing out, sparking a determined march *en masse* northward to Kensington. Under American flags fluttering in the wind as the riled-up marchers advanced, the mob was determined to exact revenge subsequent to the murder of the martyred Shiffler. This time the immigrant community was overwhelmed by the onslaught. A twenty-two-page pamphlet published shortly after the events laid out a detailed rundown of the incident. Composed as a Nativist tract, the text gave detailed descriptions of what in effect was a two-day violent street brawl. During the two-day period of rioting, May 7th to May 8th, Saint Michael's Church, the Hibernia Hose Company's firehouse, and the Nanny Goat market were burned to the ground, along with more than sixty homes, including that of alderman Hugh Clark. It is estimated that upwards of twenty people were killed. The text of the pamphlet identified many of the Nativist casualties by name, but did not personalize the "alien" ones. The rioting, which eventually spread to other neighborhoods such as the Northern Liberties and Southwark (Saint Augustine Church in the Northern Liberties was also torched and reduced to ashes), was brought under control only when the state militia was called in.

In the aftermath of the riots, various measures were taken to ensure that there would never be a repetition of such violence. The Catholic hierarchy in Philadelphia abandoned its attempt to obtain an exemption for Catholic schoolchildren from reading the Bible from the King James version. The hierarchy determined to establish its own Catholic school system—ideally an elementary school at each parish—which would guarantee a Catholic education for every Catholic school child—free of cost.

This project proceeded very successfully. The pledge of a free Catholic education for every school child remained in effect for over one hundred years. Furthermore, as the Philadelphia Church Project points out, the diocese incorporated design features for churches constructed during the ensuing decades in order that the buildings be more defendable.[28] The Basilica of St. Peter and Paul on Logan Square has minimal fenestration, while St. Anne's church on East Lehigh Avenue is characterized on the Philly Church website as a "fortress of faith" built to withstand assaults. For its part, the municipal government of Philadelphia was fed up with the hooliganism in neighboring Kensington which poured over into the city. It engineered a consolidation in 1854, making Kensington a Philadelphia neighborhood and enabling the city to more effectively police such eruptions of violence.

The first municipal election after the consolidation marked the apogee of the political power of the Know-Nothing movement in Philadelphia when Robert T. Conrad was elected mayor—the Whig candidate backed by the Know-Nothing Party. Law and order represented the keynote of Conrad's campaign. The new mayor determined to act to prevent a repetition of the violence that erupted in Kensington in 1844. He also sought to subdue the rampant hooliganism of street gangs such as the Moyamensing Killers, the Bleeders, the Blood Tubs, the Deathfetchers, the Gumballs, the Hyenas, the Smashers, the Tormentors, and others, who "battled each other for territorial rights on street corners, mauled and terrorized passersby, and covered walls and fences with graffiti."[29] He expanded the police force to 900 men, consisting exclusively of the native-born.

At the same time, he was resolved to enforce the so-called "Sunday Blue Laws" in an effort apparently directed against what was regarded by the Protestant community as the desecration of Sunday by Catholic immigrants. Included in the campaign to preserve the inviolability of the Sabbath was a ban on liquor sales as well as a ban on the circulation of newspapers. According to one commentator, eruptions of violence did not necessarily decrease, but its pattern tended to shift, as the policies introduced by Conrad "touched off a number of boisterous scuffles between citizens and police—the more boisterous because the police themselves were recruited from the kind of toughs who came out of the street gangs and were accustomed to beating up Irishmen and blacks. The early police specialized in legalized violence as their weapon against the unlegalized kind."[30]

The American Party suffered a decline as war clouds gathered during the course of the 1850s. Amid the acrimonious debates which unfolded over the issue of slavery and as the nation slid into civil war, the nativist antipathy to immigrants from Catholic countries was moved to the back burner. When the Civil War erupted in 1861, immigrants began filling the ranks of the combatants on both sides of the conflict, and engagement in combat has a wonderful way of bringing about a reordering of priorities on the part of those occupied in such life-or-death circumstances. The origins or religious affiliations of one's comrades-in-arms fade into irrelevance when bullets are flying in the midst of battle.

Nativist ire towards immigrants may have subsided on the eve of the Civil War, but the riots in Kensington should in no way be seen as a historical aberration. Nativism, of which Know-Nothingism was but one expression, runs through American history like a steady geothermal undercurrent ready to erupt at moments of demographic shifts. Nativist themes represent a consistent thread, characterized by partiality to the "native-born," particularly those of white, Anglo ancestry, and a brief excursus into that theme will demonstrate the point.

During the late 19th century and early 20th century, a convulsion of paranoia was brought about by fear of the so-called "yellow peril." Accompanying that unabashedly racist crusade was a campaign led by the patrician senator of Massachusetts, Henry Cabot Lodge, to impose restrictions upon all non-Nordic immigrants. The campaign succeeded in establishing a tight quota upon arrivals from across the Pacific. Lodge, who served in the United States Senate from 1893 to 1924, was one of the great sponsors of the cult of WASP (White, Anglo-Saxon, Protestant) superiority. In a speech he delivered in 1896, he proposed the establishment of what he termed an "illiteracy test," which, he explained, would "bear most heavily upon the Italians, Russians, Poles, Hungarians, Greeks, and Asiatics. In other words, the races most affected by the illiteracy test are those whose emigration to this country has begun within the last twenty years and swelled rapidly to enormous proportions. These races with which the English-speaking people have never hitherto assimilated, are most alien to the great body of the people of the United States. On the other hand, immigrants from the U. K. and of those races most closely related to the English-speaking people, and who with the English-speaking people themselves founded the American colonies and built up the United States, are affected little by the proposed test. Illiteracy runs parallel with the slum population, with criminals, paupers, and juvenile delinquents of foreign birth and parentage."[31] Lodge's xenophobic credo is only one manifestation of a recurrent motif in American history whereby, in order to gain support for obstructing the influx of immigrants, immigrants are demonized as being bearers of subversion and crime.

The contemporary anti-immigrant narrative focuses upon arrivals, many from Latino countries that are often conceived of as belonging to the third world, who are characterized by some with language such as: "They're bringing drugs, they're bringing crime, they're rapists." In many respects, such contemporary migration of those seeking refuge in the United States is the legacy of the bygone era of Western colonialism, when Western powers established empires and exercised economic domination on other continents. Often left in the wake of the disengagement of Western powers—a disengagement generally brought on as the result of independence movements in the colonies—were fractured societies faced with having to cope with a history of exploitation at the hands of those Western nations. To those of the WASP class in the United States, the great menace represented by these present-day migrants is melanin. However much dark skin pigmentation is upsetting to those who are the adherents of the WASP cult, Latinos have been occupying a significant place in the economic life of contemporary America, just as those poor "Romish" migrants from Ireland and Germany played a crucial role in the transformation of America into an economic powerhouse. Traditionally, the attitude towards immigration has been represented in the iconic words inscribed on the Statue of Liberty: "Give me your tired, your poor, your huddled masses yearning to breathe free." If such a solicitation has brought more diversity to American shores, such diversity and the ability of American democracy to accommodate it bear witness to a fundamental feature of the strength of the American adventure. The Nativist counter-narrative, generally constructed traditionally by that group which views itself as being owed some special status or privilege, features such measures as building walls and issuing travel bans. It remains to be seen whether such measures can stem demographic trends and check the perceived threat to the privileged status of the WASP cult represented by these less pale-skinned populations.

CHAPTER 10

AFTERMATH OF THE RIOTS: THE NEW SAINT MICHAEL'S

The St. Michael's community wasted no time recovering from the Nativist aggression of 1844. The cornerstone for a new St. Michael's church was laid in 1846, and St. Michael's Elementary School opened in 1853. In addition to those educational facilities, occupying the St. Michael's parish compound was, and is, a cemetery.

The cemetery is a rather diminutive plot of ground behind the church building and it borders Hancock Street on the east. The cemetery has long since reached capacity. Most of the sun-bleached and eroded headstones, having settled into the ground at odd angles, are unreadable, but the cemetery's website maintains a record of those interred therein.[32]

Notable on the rolls of the interred is a preponderance of Irish immigrants, not unexpectedly, as well as dozens of graves of children in the age range of ten to the late teens. All of these children died on July 17th, 1856. On that day, a train departed from the Cohocksink Depot, just a block or two west of Saint Michael's, carrying over 1,000 parishioners. Most of the passengers were children of Saint Michael's religious education program and their chaperones bound for an excursion to a suburban picnic grove in Montgomery County. Steam locomotives represented the cutting edge in modern transportation in the first half of the 19th century. As a hub of industrialization and as a growing population center, Kensington streets acquired a good deal of rail track, and until recently much of it remained embedded in Kensington streets long after the rail lines became defunct. There must have been considerable excitement among the St. Michael's school children on that hot July morning as they gathered at the rail depot. It is likely that few, if any, had ever experienced a rail outing before. If anything could inspire awe at that moment in history, it certainly was a steam locomotive with its boiler hissing and its chimney belching clouds of steam as it proceeded to chug thunderously along at the brisk speed of 35 mph.

The departure of the train was delayed almost thirty minutes owing to the time it took to board over 1,000 passengers. There would be a southbound train scheduled to depart from the northern terminus of the line in Montgomery County early that morning, but the engineer of the northbound train carrying the picnickers was confident that he could pull off onto a sidetrack in order to allow the southbound train to pass. That is, the rail line was single-track, with intermittent sidings. Due to the delayed departure from the Cohocksink depot, the engineer stepped up the speed as he pulled out of the station. He felt confident that he would detect the southbound train in the distance in time to move onto a siding. Fatefully, the opposing trains approached a blind curve simultaneously, allowing for visual contact only after it was too late. The trains collided head-on, the boilers exploding and setting off a fire in the largely wooden cars. Those in the several lead cars had no chance, the majority of them being burned alive in the ensuing conflagration. Many of those bodies were charred beyond recognition. The fatalities numbered over sixty. Almost all were students in their teens. The engineer of the northbound train perished in the accident, while the engineer of the southbound train survived the accident but reportedly took his own life that night by ingesting arsenic.

The bishop of Philadelphia, John Neumann, was out of town on visitation to several of the outlying districts of the diocese. Upon hearing the news of the accident, he rushed back to the city to minister to the grieving families. In the aftermath of the tragedy, demands for better safety measures quickly arose. Measures included that single track rail lines never be used simultaneously by trains traveling in opposite directions, and that new technology, such as the telegraph, be used so that communication could take place between train stations. Details of the accident are provided in the July 18th edition of the New York Times, 1856.[33] Ballads were composed to commemorate some of the victims, such as one commemorating Annie Lilly, age 16.

Less lamentable developments took place on the St. Michael's compound following the tragedy of 1856. The Christian Brothers appeared on the scene in 1863, opening a college on the St. Michael's compound named after the founder of the Christian Brothers, Jean Baptiste de La Salle. Ultimately, La Salle University would find a more spacious location at 20th Street and Olney Avenue in north central Philadelphia. The parish elementary school shut its doors in 2002 consequent to a steady decline in enrollment numbers. Soon thereafter, the LaSalle Academy of Philadelphia was launched, utilizing the convent on 2nd Street that housed the community of sisters that had staffed the St. Michael's school. The school operates with a census of approximately one hundred students, and exists "for parents and guardians of children who desire but cannot afford a Catholic education."[34] In addition to the LaSalle Academy elementary school, another newcomer to the St Michael's compound is the Pig Iron School. Occupying the former St. Michael's elementary school building, the Pig Iron School offers postgraduate programs and workshops in the performing arts.

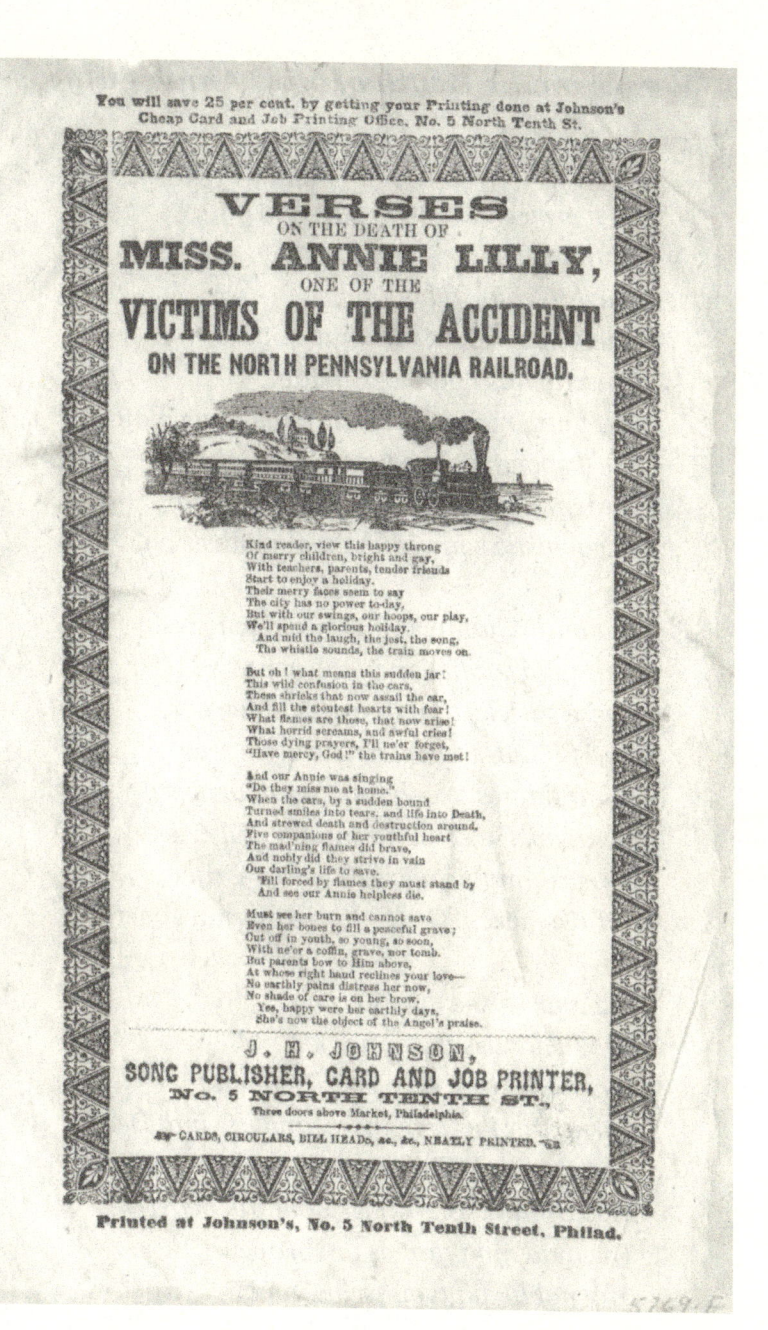

You will save 25 per cent. by getting your Printing done at Johnson's Cheap Card and Job Printing Office, No. 5 North Tenth St.

VERSES
ON THE DEATH OF
MISS. ANNIE LILLY,
ONE OF THE
VICTIMS OF THE ACCIDENT
ON THE NORTH PENNSYLVANIA RAILROAD.

Kind reader, view this happy throng
Of merry children, bright and gay,
With teachers, parents, tender friends
Start to enjoy a holiday.
   Their merry faces seem to say
   The city has no power to-day.
   But with our swings, our hoops, our play,
   We'll spend a glorious holiday.
     And mid the laugh, the jest, the song,
     The whistle sounds, the train moves on.

But oh! what means this sudden jar!
This wild confusion in the cars,
These shrieks that now assail the ear,
And fill the stoutest hearts with fear!
What flames are those, that now arise!
What horrid screams, and awful cries!
Those dying prayers, I'll ne'er forget,
"Have mercy, God!" the trains have met!

And our Annie was singing
"Do they miss me at home."
When the cars, by a sudden bound
Turned smiles into tears, and life into Death,
And strewed death and destruction around.
Five companions of her youthful heart
The mad'ning flames did brave,
And nobly did they strive in vain
Our darling's life to save.
   Till forced by flames they must stand by
   And see our Annie helpless die.

Must see her burn and cannot save
Even her bones to fill a peaceful grave;
Cut off in youth, so young, so soon,
With ne'er a coffin, grave, nor tomb.
But parents bow to Him above,
At whose right hand reclines your love—
No earthly pains distress her now,
No shade of care is on her brow,
Yes, happy were her earthly days,
She's now the object of the Angel's praise.

J. H. JOHNSON,
SONG PUBLISHER, CARD AND JOB PRINTER,
No. 5 NORTH TENTH ST.,
Three doors above Market, Philadelphia.

CARDS, CIRCULARS, BILL HEADS, &c., &c., NEATLY PRINTED.

Printed at Johnson's, No. 5 North Tenth Street, Philad.

Courtesy of the Library Company of Philadelphia

Charles Lutz

Verses on the Death of Miss Annie Lilly

Kind reader, view this happy throng
Of merry children, bright and gay,
With teachers, parents, tender friends
Start to enjoy a holiday.
Their merry faces seem to say
The city has no power today.
But with our swings, our hopes, our play,
We'll spend a glorious holiday.
And mid the laugh, the jest, the song,
The whistle sounds, the train moves on.

But oh! What means this sudden jar!
This wild confusion in the cars,
These shrieks that now assail the ear,
And fill the stoutest hearts with fear!
What flames are those, that now arise!
What horrid screams, and awful cries!
Those dying prayers, I'll ne'er forget,
 "Have mercy, God!" the trains have met!

And our Annie was singing
"Do they miss me at home?"
When the cars, by a sudden bound
Turned smiles into tears, and life into Death,
And strewed death and destruction around.
Five companions of her youthful heart
The mad'ning flames did brave,
And nobly did they strive in vain

Our darling's life to save.
 'Till forced by flames they must stand by
And see our Annie helpless die.

Must see her burn and cannot save
Even her bones to fill a peaceful grave;
Cut off in youth, so young, so soon,
With ne'er a coffin, grave, nor tomb.
But parents bow to Him above,
At whose right hand reclines your love—
No earthly pains distress her now.
No shades of care is on her brow.
Yes, happy were her earthly days,
She's now the object of the Angel's praise.

PART III:

JOHN NEUMANN

CHAPTER 11

THE NEUMANN SHRINE AT ST. PETER'S

Continuing to proceed south below Saint Michael's church along 2nd Street, one reaches the putative southern boundary of Kensington, viz., Girard Avenue—the boundary separating Kensington from the Northern Liberties. If the neighborhood of which Saint Michael's is the center constituted the Irish enclave, Saint Peter's church at 5th and Girard stood at the heart of the German quarter. The parish, established in 1843 to serve the growing numbers of German Catholic immigrants was, and is, staffed by the Congregation of the Holy Redeemer, or more commonly, the Redemptorists. In 1844 the church building, then still under construction, was left unmolested by the nativist rioters as they advanced south towards other targets. It may be supposed that they had no beef with the Germans.

Saint Peter's church has been a site of pilgrimage since in its lower church is enshrined the remains of Saint John Neumann—a member of the Redemptorist Order who served as Philadelphia's fourth bishop from 1852 until his death in 1860. If the drama of Kensington's history has tended to unfold with a paucity of famous personages, at least here at 5th and Girard lies the remains of a saint—a saint who, in fact, requested that his final resting place be that community in Kensington where he did not feel out of place—Saint Peter's. Being declared venerable in 1921 and beatified in 1963—two steps in the process of being declared a saint—he was canonized in 1977. More than a few parishes across the nation now bear the name Saint John Neumann, and an online search reveals fourteen high schools across the country named for John Neumann, plus a Saint John Neumann High School in Budweis, Czech Republic. In addition, there is a Neumann University just south of Philadelphia in Aston, PA.

Saint Peter's church was set amidst several prominent Kensington landmarks, viz., the Schmidt's brewery on 2nd Street east of the church and the Stetson hat factory complex, which occupied a campus of several acres a stone's throw from the church on the north side of Girard Avenue. While the Schmidt's brewery and the Stetson hat factory closed shop in the final decades of the 20th century and whose buildings soon afterwards succumbed to the wrecking ball, Saint Peter's church has continued to command the airspace over the neighborhood by virtue of its tall, pointed spire. For most of the 20th century, a modest sign posted at the entrance to the lower church beckoned passersby inside to pay their respects to the Venerable John Neumann. In recent years, since canonization, there has been considerable upgrading of the shrine and alteration of the ambience—changes consequent to the canonization of the bishop as well as to shifts in religious tastes that have unfolded since the 2nd Vatican Council.

Initially entombed in the undercroft of the lower church, the remains of the bishop were put on display to public view following his beatification in a glass crypt in front of the main altar. The remains are encased in a recumbent effigy clothed in a bishop's habiliment, which, for many observers, due to the lifelike appearance of the form, gives rise to questions as to whether the body perhaps did not corrupt. It did. Such is reported on the website of the Redemptorists' monthly publication, the Liguorian: "The saint's remains are enclosed in glass below the main altar of the shrine church. The saint's body is not incorrupt. The remains are covered by a mask that faithfully represents the saint's face and by a bishop's vestments."[35]

For a young walker having arrived at the endpoint of a walk-through Kensington, this terminus merited substantial ruminations. Who is this person being so exalted as to have his body placed on public display? How is it that Kensington, not known as a locale rich with monuments to historically prominent dignitaries, has been so honored?

In the midst of a neighborhood environment where the wheels of industry were churning out hosiery or carpets and whatever other textiles, here was a space, that of the lower church of Saint Peter's, of mystery and otherworldliness. In the 1950s the dimly lit space was claustrophobic, with its low, flat ceiling and the air permeated with the smell of incense. The eyes were immediately drawn to the venerable Neumann, who, though having died in the middle of the 19th century, appeared whole as the bier on which his body was laid out stood positioned before the main altar. Another altar, that of St. Joseph to the right of the bier, displayed a collection of human bones within its glass-enclosed frame. These, presumably, were holy relics brought from Europe by those largely European-born Redemptorists who staffed Saint Peter's during the first hundred years of its existence. If the effect was macabre, the veneration of relics was a significant feature of the piety of immigrants from the Old World served by Saint Peter's for many generations during the 19th and early 20th centuries. The evocation of life after death did not end there. To the left of the sanctuary was a small room—a mini-museum—exhibiting items of significance to the life of Neumann. Here one could gaze upon the slab of marble stoop on which the apoplexy-stricken Neumann collapsed, when walking along Vine Street while carrying out an errand on Thursday, January 5th, 1860. On display as well was a black hood and noose, the grim accessories of the execution of the Skupinski brothers—Matthias and Blaise—carried out at the Philadelphia County Prison, aka the Moyamensing Prison, in 1852. The two Polish-born brothers having been convicted of bludgeoning to death a jewelry salesman named Jacob Lehman and consigned to death row shortly after Neumann's arrival in Philadelphia as the city's new bishop, it was one of Neumann's first pastoral initiatives to call upon the incarcerated brothers, who apparently had been declining the ministrations of a priest, and urge them to be reconciled with God before their date with the hangman. Neumann succeeded in obtaining their agreement to his counsel and a Neumann-appointed chaplain, accompanying the felons to gallows, was able to bestow the last rites during their final moments. The grisly mementos—hood and noose—of the incident were presented to the bishop and their exposition in the museum immortalizes the story for the visitor to the shrine and contributed to the eerie atmosphere of the museum, at least that of the pre-updated museum.

 Since the 2nd Vatican Council held in the early 1960s, the Neumann shrine has undergone a makeover whereby the former gloom and otherworldly ambience of the shrine has given way to a brighter, more buoyant space. Amid the lighter-colored pews and the brighter lighting, the focus remains the body of a saint—John Neumann. Gone from view are the assortment of saints' bones and other relics. The mini-museum which was housed in the small room beside the sanctuary has been moved into a more expanded space, more elaborately celebrating Neumann's life and the times in which he lived. But just what is it that Neumann did, what is it about his life, that merits special veneration?

Kensington Chronicles

> Neumann was always eager to encourage people to join him in the cause of religion. The Church had a long tradition of turning to religious communities of men and women to seek out society's most vulnerable for the provision of God's love. He warmly encouraged and fostered religious life in the diocese.

A SHORT BIOGRAPHICAL SKETCH OF JOHN NEUMANN

In the summer of 1853, about a year and a half into Neumann's episcopate as bishop of Philadelphia, Gaetano Cardinal Bedini, a seasoned diplomat who served the papacy during the 1840s and 1850s, arrived in New York City in order to make the rounds of various dioceses of the United States. It would be the first time that a Papal nuncio visited the United States. He had a lengthy to- do list during his six-month stay, on which was included the task of getting to the bottom of the reputed discontent in Philadelphia towards the bishop there, that is, towards John Neumann. Bedini had to carry out his mission amid continual uproar stemming from the anti-Papal camp, which comprised not only nativists who were alarmed over Catholic immigration into the U. S. but also emigres having fled from Europe after the failed 1848 insurrections. It may be remembered that Bedini was a representative not only of the spiritual head of the Catholic Church but also of the autocratic monarch who ruled the Papal States, that anti-democratic bulwark standing in the way of revolutionary attempts to create a democratic state on the Italian peninsula. The cardinal's life was most in danger in Cincinnati, Ohio, where apparently a significant population of central European émigrés had settled—

escapees whose lives were at risk following the failure of their insurrection. Armed demonstrators organized a protest march and proceeded to advance upon the bishop's residence in Cincinnati where Bedini was lodging. The police, determined to halt the progress of the march, charged the demonstrators and, in the melee that ensued, one was killed and approximately twenty were wounded. Bedini was successfully hustled out of the city to safety. When he completed his rounds of American dioceses in January of 1854 and was ready to commence his return to Rome from New York City, he had to be smuggled on board his ship in New York harbor under cover of night.

Bedini was well aware of the discontent in Philadelphia, as grumblings about Bishop Neumann had found their way to Rome, largely consisting of doubts about Neumann's fitness for the post of bishop. Many, perhaps most, of Neumann's detractors were priests of the diocese, as well as several fellow American bishops. An excerpt from Bedini's final report to the Pope runs as follows:

"The Bishop of Philadelphia seems a little inferior for the importance of such a distinguished city, not in learning or in zeal nor in piety, but because of the littleness of his person and his neglect of the fashions.

He is indeed very holy and full of zeal, but more as a missionary than a bishop. He is not able to forget the very humble customs of the order to which he belongs (the Redemptorists), but the populous city of Philadelphia, rich, intelligent, full of life and importance, surely merits a bishop of another type."[36]

Since Neumann was neither transferred elsewhere nor was he removed from the post of bishop outright, it can be presumed that the Pope was unimpressed with the suggestion that Neumann lacked sufficient height to be bishop (Neumann reportedly was five feet two inches) or that his apparel was deficient in stylishness. It is very likely true that Neumann was attached to the "customs" of his order, although the word "customs" seems an odd choice of a word to characterize the evangelical vows of poverty, chastity, and obedience. It is likely as well that Neumann indicated to Bedini that he would welcome a transfer to a "less cultured" diocese. But the question arises: how did Neumann come to be bishop in the first place?

Neumann grew up in a devout Catholic family in the German-speaking region of Bohemia, located currently in the Czech Republic, which during the time of Neumann was part of the Austrian Empire, ruled by the Hapsburg dynasty. Upon completing his seminary studies in Budweis—a city which would later give its name to a popular American beer—he learned that there was a moratorium in his diocese on ordinations, owing to a surplus of priests. However, he had already been entertaining thoughts of doing missionary work in the United States. In particular, he fantasized about doing missionary work among the indigenous people of the U.S. He dropped hints about this to his family as well as to several of his classmates, though it seems that it remained unclear to his family just how serious these plans were. Meanwhile, Neumann applied for a passport and had obtained some financial backing through a local bishop. When the passport arrived—approximately six months after he had completed his seminary training—he slipped out of Prachatitz, his hometown, without a ceremonious leave-taking. Three days after his departure he sent home a letter explaining to his family that he wanted to spare them a painful farewell. At the same time he acknowledged that he wanted to spare himself as well.

Despite very meager financial resources he found his way to La Havre, France, where he boarded the sailing vessel Europa in April, 1836, for the transatlantic voyage, which would take, symbolically, forty days. He had virtually no money, one set of clothing, was unordained, and was thrown among a crowd of total strangers. Also, he had left with no so-called dimissorial papers, that is, formal permission from the bishop of his diocese releasing him from serving in the diocese which had underwritten his seminary education. While he had several letters of recommendation, the lack of dimissorial papers would later vex his rather scrupulous conscience.

Upon landing in New York City, he wandered the streets of Manhattan, which boasted at that time a population of approximately 300,000, trying to hunt down a Catholic church. Fortuitously, despite minimal financial resources and limited English, he found his way to the residence of the bishop of New York, John Dubois, a Parisian-born French émigré who, disinclined to embrace the French revolution, had fled to the United States in 1791. The bishop, being in acute need of German- speaking priests, enthusiastically welcomed Neumann, who, armed with at least several letters of recommendation, was ordained by DuBois at the New York cathedral within a month of his arrival. Upon ordination, Neumann was peremptorily shipped out to the hinterland of western New York, where the city of Buffalo was beginning to beckon settlers—many from German-speaking lands—following the completion of the Erie Canal in 1825. While at that time Buffalo had a population of close to 16,000, Neumann's beat would comprise a broad swath of territory throughout the surrounding exurbs of Buffalo. Neumann was finally realizing his dream of providing pastoral care to a community of simple, hard-working immigrants.

The challenges which Neumann would face were substantial. The source which provides an account of Neumann's experiences during his first pastoral assignment is that of Neumann's earliest biographer, his nephew John Berger, who arrived in America from Bohemia in 1857 to begin studies for the priesthood.[37] Being able to enjoy occasional visits with his uncle, as well as accumulating much anecdotal material from acquaintances of Neumann over the course of many years, Berger stored up a significant amount of material relevant for his biography. Berger's chapter covering his uncle's four years in western New York shows that Neumann was put to the test both physically and emotionally. The communities that he served were spread over an extensive stretch of territory. The terrain was harsh, and there were few roads. Winters in western New York are characterized by snowstorms of monumental proportions, and the spring thaw brings swampy conditions at best and occasional flooding at worst. Mosquitos were a novelty to Neumann and were a relentless torment. In terms of mobility, he had to make the circuit of his extensive territory on foot or, despite poor equestrian skills in the estimation of Berger, on the back of a horse.

Neumann also had to contend with the climate of increasing hostility towards Catholics in the wake of Catholic immigration from Ireland and Germany. Western New York at the time was in the grip of the so-called Second Great Awakening, and the number and intensity of religious revivals which took place there earned western New York the designation, the "burned-out district." During the first half of the nineteenth century millenialist groups emerged, such as the Millerites—followers of William Miller, whose brand of Christianity was characterized by the practice of predicting the date, or the revised dates, of the end-time and 2nd coming of Christ (it goes without saying that the end of time never took place). The roots of Mormonism—Joseph Smith claimed to have found the golden plates on which were transcribed the Book of Mormon on a hillside in Manchester, New York, just south of Rochester—as well as the roots of the Seventh-Day Adventist church, are found in this region, which was fiercely afire with religious ardor. The era of interfaith rapprochement still being over a century away, Catholics were seen as being hopelessly ensnared in darkness and superstition, while Protestants were viewed by Catholics as being perverted by heresy. Berger characterizes Neumann's indefatigable zeal in ministering to the German community scattered throughout this extensive region as being fueled by his determination to prevent any defection of Catholics to any of these Protestant sects. Berger quotes a letter of Neumann's in which his uncle leaves little doubt of his distaste towards these diverse sects: "Their noisy preaching in the streets and public places, the obtrusiveness of those who distribute Bibles, their ridiculous prophecies respecting the Day of Judgment, etc., amaze us Catholics; . . . [during religious services] all are praying aloud, though not in concert. One shouts, another screams; some weep, some sing; whilst others, turning deadly pale, fall to the floor, foam at the mouth, groan as if in agony, roll about convulsively, having, as they blasphemously assert, received the Holy Ghost."[38] The times being what they were, the tightly circumscribed understanding of religious experience held by Neumann was not something he could easily transcend.

The territory assigned to Neumann measured some 900 square miles, and of service to the faithful in that extensive region were four church buildings, miles apart from one another, in various stages of incompletion. Neumann opted to operate out of the most centrally located of these churches, in the town of Williamsville, located several miles to the northeast of the center of Buffalo. There was no rectory, so Neumann was lodged in the home of a parishioner. The church building being as yet without a roof, all liturgical services were open to the sky. Derisive taunts shouted by passersby could at times be heard by those in attendance at Mass, and on occasion a rock, tossed by some passing hooligan, would crash down upon the congregation.

Eventually, Neumann was provided a modest rectory—a two-room log cabin made available to Neumann by a parishioner of the North Bush parish community. Neumann's physically grueling regimen of trekking from church to church remained unaltered. That, coupled with a spirituality in which self-mortification was a significant feature, conspired to place a serious strain on Neumann's constitution. Berger, whose method does not divert from that of traditional Catholic hagiography, writes admiringly of his uncle's austere habits, and his edifying portrait of Neumann concedes nothing that may suggest the slightest blemish in Neumann's character. Neumann's diet and sleep habits were Spartan, to put it lightly. If Berger's account is accurate, Neumann generally slept no more than a couple of hours per night, often preferring the hard floor over the use of his bed. He would go for days on a diet of bread and coffee, a regimen only on occasion interrupted when invited into a parishioner's home for dinner, "so he could enjoy good food properly prepared."[39] What hearth he had usually went untouched: "scarcely once a week was smoke seen to rise from the chimney."[40] His ascetic lifestyle did not fail to include practices of self-mortification, and mortification "of the flesh" was not omitted, as Berger reports: "he wore a girdle of iron wire that penetrated the flesh; he chastised his innocent body with a scourge which he had armed with a sharp nail."[41]

Consequent to his physically demanding regimen of incessant trekking, on foot or at times on horseback, from one church community to another, along with his ascetical habits, he found himself in 1840 "completely broken down," in the words of his nephew,[42] and was laid up for three months with a recalcitrant fever, severe bronchitis, and overall physical collapse. His "pristine vigor was gone," writes Berger, and his "delicate health dates from that period." Neumann is reputed to have said to a fellow priest, Alexander Pax, who had been Neumann's confessor: "Father Pax, I must give up; my health is gone."

It was at that moment that Neumann decided to seek admission into the Congregation of the Most Holy Redeemer, better known as the Redemptorists. His friend Alexander Pax had urged him to consider admission into a community such as the Redemptorists, as a means to countervail the isolation that he was having to endure. Unsurprisingly, his bishop, John Hughes, was reluctant to lose someone who was conscientious, dependable, and who could speak German, stalled for time but was ultimately required, by Canon Law, to accede to Neumann's wishes. In October of 1840 Neumann departed from New York and headed to Pittsburgh, where was located the central Redemptorist house at which Neumann would begin his year-long novitiate, that is, a year of spiritual formation and orientation to the particular métier of the Redemptorist order.

Neumann was likely cherishing the prospect of an extended period of prayer, meditation, and spiritual reading—a welcome respite following the punishing years spent in the notorious snow belt of western New York. But it was not to be. The Redemptorists were spread thin and had taken on so many assignments across the country that there was slim chance that Neumann would be able to chill out for a year in prayerful tranquility. Throughout the year he was moved around no fewer than eight times to perform pastoral duties in various far-flung locales. He is known to have said on several occasions that he never really had a novitiate. At times he wondered if he was really wanted, filling in briefly in one place before being shuffled off elsewhere. According to his biographers, he at times questioned whether he had made the correct decision opting to enter the Redemptorists. In one of his temporary assignments in southern Ohio, the bishop there, John Purcell, pressured him to join the diocese of Cincinnati. Apparently his Redemptorist superiors recognized the problem and eventually decided to assign him a 5-week respite from pastoral duties. Finally, in January of 1842, he was professed as a Redemptorist.

Once being formally inducted into the Redemptorists, Neumann was plunged into pastoral work, which likely was a great relief to him, as that was what he had wanted all along. He was assigned to operate out of Saint James parish in Baltimore, MD, to serve the ever-growing population of German immigrants there. A new church—Saint Alphonsus— was under construction, which would be larger and more resplendent than Saint James. Hopefully the Germans, with their reputation for querulousness, would be gratified with the new church. As Irish-born bishops seemed to predominate in the American hierarchy, the Germans often complained of being neglected. There was a suspicion on the part of the Germans that monies sent from societies such as the Vienna-based Leopoldine Society to aid German immigrants in the U.S. were not always used to benefit the German community. For this reason, the Redemptorists, who were largely German-speaking, were highly sought after to relieve bishops of having to deal directly with the problems stemming from the discontent of the Germans. Presumably owing to an abundance of missionary zeal, the Redemptorists tended to overextend themselves and assume projects for which funds were inadequate to handle. The Redemptorist order being managed from across the ocean, the zeal of the Redemptorist missionaries in the expansive territory of the United States tended to outpace the financial means of the order.

Amid the turmoil brought about by the Redemptorists in the

U.S. undertaking ventures beyond the ability of the order to keep up financially, Neumann went about devoting all his energy to pastoral work. That is, until 1847. He was informed, rather unexpectedly, that he was appointed superior of the Order in the U.S. He would be answerable to the Order's Superior-General in Europe and was essentially charged with reducing debts and reining in those in the Order who, in their excess of eagerness, were taking on endless financial burdens. It did not seem like a coveted assignment, at least for someone like Neumann for whom pastoral work was his element. The two-year period during which Neumann held this office was highly stressful and there were grumblings in the ranks about Neumann's difficulties exercising authority. In 1848, after Neumann's first year as Superior, the Superior-General in Europe—one Michael Heilig— communicated to him the following: "I cannot conceal from you, and I believe Your Reverence freely admits it, that you have to contend with strong opposition from our men in America."[43] Tell me something I don't know, we can imagine Neumann thinking. Neumann had, in fact, made known to headquarters in Europe the difficulties that he was experiencing, and on more than one occasion had offered to resign. Trying to be supportive but likely feeling rather frustrated, the Superior-General offered the following: "Although Your Reverence complains very much about the portion of the congregation under your care and direction and you sigh under the burden you bear, I am, nevertheless, satisfied with what your letters reveal and glad that you have no complaints about more and weightier matters . . . Let us thank God that matters are not worse than they are. I hope Your Reverence will regain your composure and willingly bear the hardships that obedience imposes on you."[44] (Chapter viii of Curley's biography features substantial correspondence between Neumann and his superior in Europe). Neumann's European

Superior was not inclined to accept Neumann's offer of resignation, and Neumann continued soldiering along despite the persistent administrative headaches which he apparently felt ill-suited to deal with.

According to Curley's biography, Neumann's supporters urged him to fight back against his detractors, but Neumann brushed aside these suggestions: "I have never done anything to become Superior and I will not do anything to remain one. On the contrary, I will thank God if I am relieved of this responsibility."

Neumann continued in his post until January, 1849, at which time his Superior in Europe finally ceased his efforts to buoy up Neumann with words of encouragement and acceded to his wish to be replaced. While Neumann thereupon assumed the role of simple parish curate in Baltimore, he was appointed "consultant" of the new Superior. The next three years would provide a bit of a respite from administrative headaches. Not only was he able to devote more time to pastoral work, but he also found time to compose a catechism (Katholischer Katechismus) while contributing articles on theological topics to the local Catholic newspaper in Baltimore, the Katholische Kirchenzeitung. But this 3-year period of relative serenity would not last.

In the Fall of 1851, Francis Kenrick, bishop of Philadelphia, was appointed archbishop of Baltimore. This was a promotion. As the first diocese to be established in the United States, Baltimore was, and is, the premier see of the United States. During his initial months in his new post, Kenrick became acquainted with Neumann, stationed in the new Saint Alphonsus parish several blocks away from the Baltimore Cathedral where Kenrick resided. In effect, Neumann became Kenrick's confessor and Kenrick got to know Neumann fairly well and was impressed with Neumann's intelligence and saintliness.

Of the important tasks confronting Kenrick was the matter of recommending to Rome his successor for the post of bishop of Philadelphia. In his interactions with Neumann Kenrick began dropping hints that he might be shortlisted for the job of bishop of Philadelphia. In light of Neumann's temperament and the vexation that he experienced as the Superior of the Redemptorists in the United States, he can only have been deeply alarmed at the prospect of being invested as bishop of one of the largest dioceses in the United States. Something obviously impressed Kenrick about Neumann, likely his piety, conscientiousness, good sense, and, without question, his ability to speak German. Fatefully, Neumann was indeed selected to become bishop of Philadelphia. According to Curley's account, on the eve of his consecration in March, 1852, Neumann is said to have lamented to a confrere: "I'd rather die tomorrow than be consecrated bishop."

Neumann held the post of bishop of Philadelphia until his death in 1860. At the time of his elevation to the episcopate, there were those who expressed doubts about his fitness for the post, albeit his piety and conscientiousness always seemed to be acknowledged. What did these doubts consist of? Neumann's nephew, John Berger, addresses the question in his characteristic hagiographic style. First of all, notes Berger, the task of easily recognizing Neumann's saintly deeds was made difficult by virtue of his uncle's humility: "For although the servant of God performed many great deeds, his extraordinary humility enabled him to conceal them, in a measure, from the eyes of all save God alone."[45] In the chapter entitled, "Some Traits of Bishop Neumann's Saintly Character," is found much anecdotal material about the habits of the bishop.[46] Much of the material strikes some notes of awkwardness and amusement,

Neumann being, at least as far as he was concerned, an unlikely candidate for the exalted office such as that of a bishop. For example, there seemed to be some annoyance on the part of some on the bishop's staff towards his deportment. A Father Bach once confronted the bishop: "Bishop, you look shabby. Today is Sunday. Have the goodness to change your clothes." The bishop responded that there was nothing he could do about it, as he had no other clothes. Despite being exempt from his vow of poverty by virtue of his elevation to the episcopate, Neumann never seems to have been able, or to have had the desire, to display the courtly bearing expected of a bishop.

On another occasion the same Father Bach voiced objections to Neumann about his sleeping habits. It was intimated by more than one observer that Neumann regularly neglected to use his bed, opting instead to sleep on the floor. Noticing once that Neumann was lying on a hard board on the floor of his room, Father Bach reproved such behavior forthwith: "Bishop, you ought to be in bed. You are sick." When Neumann remonstrated with his curate, Bach shot back: "You are a bishop and you are not at liberty to dispose of yourself. You belong to your diocese." Disinclined to argue with such a seemingly reasonable rejoinder, Neumann complied with Bach's behest.

If Neumann's self-abasing personality was at odds with the stereotypical image of episcopal stateliness, at least by nineteenth century standards, such incidents reported by Berger furnish much amusement. On one occasion when the Redemptorist community at Saint Peter's was ceremoniously welcoming a visiting prelate from Europe, Neumann happened to be in attendance at the event. The visiting dignitary registered Neumann's presence, though without being aware of Neumann's ecclesiastical status: "How singular!" noted the visitor; "Is this the way they do things here in America? Do they allow strangers and people of no account to enter the cloister and communicate so familiarly with the community?"[47] When the visitor was formally introduced to the bishop, the mortified visitor was obliged to re-assess his jaundiced mindset.

Perhaps the most significant source of discontent with Neumann was his alleged deficiency when it came to managing the financial affairs of the diocese. The diocese incurred considerable debt during Kenrick's watch, not the least cause of which was the uncompleted Cathedral, begun in 1846 on Logan Circle, which in fact never was completed during Neumann's tenure. Kenrick, well aware of the tenuous financial straits of the diocese he was bequeathing to Neumann, did not seem to take into account how the financial condition of the diocese would fare under Neumann's care. The priest charged with overseeing the construction of the Cathedral, only one-third completed at the time of Neumann's elevation to the episcopate, Edmund Waldron, is reported to have considered Neumann to be "completely incompetent."

Eventually some American bishops started piling on, most notably, the blunt and opinionated bishop of Pittsburgh, Michael O'Connor. To begin with, there was a paucity of good feeling held by O'Connor towards the Redemptorists, as earlier during his tenure as bishop German Catholics in his diocese forwarded complaints to Rome alleging that they were being neglected and that monies sent by the Leopoldine Society in Vienna to benefit German Catholic immigrants were being used for other purposes rather than for the welfare of the Germans. O'Connor suspected that these querulous Germans were being encouraged by the Redemptorists to report their grievances directly to Rome. At any rate, O'Connor's summation of the situation in Philadelphia included the following: "He (Neumann) is very timid, is not so well versed in the language as to be able to address the people effectively; his manners are inclined to keep him aloof from the clergy and the people, and therefore there is no love or affection toward him. Some, unjustly indeed but in truth, hold him in low esteem."[48]

Neumann's apparent deficiencies, whether having to do with his lack of money-management skills or introverted personality, did not prevent him from being remarkably productive. In the largest diocese in the United States he managed to establish approximately eighty new parishes. He was committed to the expansion of the parochial school system and insisted that each parish begin construction of a primary school. He set up a central board of education to administer what was to become the largest parochial school system in the United States. Those pastors who hesitated about adding a school to their parish, owing to the expense, were threatened by Neumann with reassignment and replacement of a pastor who would get on board with Neumann's educational policy objectives, despite whatever debts would be incurred. His alleged timidity was trumped by his insistence on this matter. Furthermore, in 1859 he opened a minor seminary in Glen Riddle, and he was quick to arrange entrance into the diocese by religious orders of sisters and brothers to staff diocesan schools as teachers and administrators—orders such as the Holy Cross sisters, the Holy Cross brothers, the sisters of Notre Dame de Namur, the Christian Brothers, among others. Finally, despite significant opposition, he went ahead with a project to construct an orphanage, to be called the Saint Vincent's Orphanage, in Tacony—a significant addition to the already monumental diocesan debt. All of these activities were exercised amid a climate bristling with criticism of the bishop.

It was Neumann's apparent lack of expertise in the management of financial matters that raised a call for quick action. Neumann himself as much as anyone admitted his shortcomings in this area—it was perhaps the chief reason why Neumann offered to be moved to a smaller diocese. The problem was effectively addressed in 1857 when a co-adjutor was assigned to the diocese of Philadelphia to assist Neumann in managing the financial affairs of the diocese. James Wood was tapped to assume that post and he contrasted sharply with Neumann in every respect. Tall, native-born, articulate and self-assured, Wood had significant banking experience in his pre-seminary life. Cardinal Bedini would likely have seen in Wood the perfect image of episcopal stateliness. James Wood grew up in a Unitarian family in Philadelphia and, when he was fourteen, he and his family moved to Cincinnati, Ohio, where, upon completing his education, he embarked on a banking career. In the course of his business-related duties he developed a friendship with the bishop of Cincinnati—John B. Purcell— and decided to convert to Catholicism. Meanwhile he acquired significant expertise in bookkeeping and in managing a variety of financial transactions—expertise which was perfectly suited to tackling the knotty financial muddle of the Philadelphia diocese.

Wood was well aware of the struggles which Neumann had been experiencing and of the deficiencies that Neumann was reported to have had regarding the exercise of authority and the management of financial affairs. He likewise was aware that Neumann had expressed a willingness, or rather an eagerness, to be moved to a smaller diocese. Apparently Wood fully expected that his role as co- adjutor was a very temporary one and that he would assume the post of bishop of Philadelphia forthwith once Neumann was settled in arrangements that would be less onerous for the unworldly bishop. Wood's expectation would remain unmet and the three years which Wood would spend as coadjutor—Neumann would die unexpectedly in January, 1860—would turn out to be a frustrating ordeal for him.

There exist letters which testify to the rather awkward drama which unfolded during the three-year period in which Wood and Neumann were thrown together. One perhaps can feel some sympathy for the vigorous Wood, who seems to have had a take-charge nature as a consequence of which a subordinate role, especially to someone whom he regarded as less than competent, was irksome. Wood maintained a correspondence with his old friend and mentor Edward Purcell, bishop of Cincinnati, in one of which he reports: "Certainly now I feel uneasy and uncertain as to the future. My venerated Senior (sic) is of a temperament which I cannot deal with, and, no doubt, without intending it makes me the victim of an anxiety which I can scarcely explain, tho I feel it deeply. Debts, debts, debts—God help me, and I am sure that you will pray that I may be faithful to His graces."[49]

In another lengthy letter which he sent to Rome to the Prefect of the Sacred Congregation of Propaganda, Alessandro Barnabo, in September, 1858, he provided essentially a report of the state of the diocese—a report which laid out a less than heartening picture. He furnishes in the letter a long list of diocesan debts, and adds that amid all these financial burdens, Neumann happened to take on an extremely expensive project to erect an orphanage (Saint Vincent's Orphan Asylum in Tacony, established in 1855). The project having been launched several years prior to Wood's appointment as coadjutor, Wood was not in a position to nix it even if he would have been able. More than likely Neumann had perceived a need for such an institution and he was not constituted to permit financial considerations to thwart the fulfillment of what he saw as an urgent need. At any rate the more provident co-adjutor paints a portrait of the bishop which is less than flattering: "I am sorry to say that there exists almost universally among the clergy an aversion to the Reverend Bishop, and little trust, little love and affection in this regard. This, however, although it is sometimes easy to see, never reaches the point where they openly oppose his dispositions; rather it causes them not to cooperate with His Lordship as one would wish. Nor can one exactly blame the Reverend Prelate for this; it follows rather as a consequence of his somewhat cold and gloomy character (he is a native of Bohemia) and of his manner of dealing with people, which does not so much conciliate as repel."[50] It is difficult to account for Wood's rather derogatory swipe at the central European territory of Bohemia, but apparently Neumann did not feel driven to make people like him, and if the stereotypical image of American demeanor includes skills in self-promotion and an aptitude for engaging in self-congratulatory palaver, Neumann's self-effacing temperament was poorly equipped to conform to that cultural ideal. Posterity is charged with trying to reconcile Wood's less than laudatory characterization of Neumann's temperament with the effusion of honor accorded to Neumann by a multitude of the faithful following his death.

No doubt Neumann welcomed the appointment of a co-adjutor and it can be easily imagined that he felt as if an immense burden had been lifted from his shoulders. Now he could spend time in the outlying, and less urban, districts of the diocese without a nagging feeling of dereliction. For Wood's part, he would only have to tolerate his irksome situation for a little more than two years, as Neumann died suddenly due to an attack of apoplexy, that is, some kind of unspecified cardiovascular event, in January of 1860, just several weeks shy of his forty-ninth birthday. Per the terms of his appointment as co-adjutor, Wood immediately took over the post of bishop of Philadelphia. If Philadelphia deserved a bishop different from Neumann, as

Cardinal Baedini had asserted, the august Wood fit the bill.

The new cathedral not having yet been completed during Neumann's tenure, Neumann's funeral was celebrated at the pro-cathedral on 13th Street—the church of Saint John the Evangelist. A vault in the burial ground next to the pro-cathedral was prepared for his body, per the directive of Bishop Wood, who refused the request of the Redemptorists that Neumann be buried at St. Peter's. However, Archbishop Kenrich, having been alerted to the Redemptorists' request, overruled Wood, paving the way for Neumann's internment at St. Peter's: "I gladly agree to have Bishop Neumann find a resting place, in death, in the place where he truly desired it in life but did not find it."[51] Neumann indeed would be interred at Saint Peter's in Kensington—the place staffed by Neumann's fellow Redemptorists and where Neumann apparently preferred spending his free time when his duties required him to be in the city. Thus would Kensington be able to lay claim to have in its precincts the burial site of a saint. Neumann would be only one of three bishops of Philadelphia not to be buried in the crypt under the main altar of the Cathedral, the others being Francis Kenrick, who is buried at the Basilica of the Assumption in Baltimore, and John O'Hara, Philadelphia's ninth bishop, who, as a member of the Congregation of the Holy Cross, is entombed at the Basilica of the Sacred Heart on the campus of the University of Notre Dame in South Bend, Indiana.

With free rein to disencumber the diocese of its financial burdens, Wood would amply prove his administrative acumen. Most notably, the cathedral on Logan Square would be completed during his tenure. But in the midst of throwing himself into the business of straightening out the diocese's woeful financial condition, Wood would witness an unexpected phenomenon which would eventually make Saint Peter's a pilgrimage destination. Large numbers of the faithful came to pray at Neumann's tomb. If Neumann failed to have star power with the gentry of the diocese, and was not always regarded highly by Church authorities, his piety and dedication to pastoral work did not go unnoticed by the common people, who came in substantial numbers to pray at his tomb. Cures were reported—cures alleged by the faithful to have been effectuated owing to Neumann's intercession. Inevitably, discussion ensued about establishing a timetable for canonization. He was declared venerable in 1921, the first step on the road to official sainthood. Canonization would take place in 1977, giving Neumann the distinction of being the first male American saint (Neumann was naturalized as an American citizen in 1848). Kensington would thereupon be blessed by the presence of a holy shrine within its precincts.

PART IV:

A THEOLOGICAL

REFLECTION

CHAPTER 13

JOHN NEUMANN AND SAINTHOOD

The Neumann shrine, as the terminus of this trek along the streets of Kensington and as a site which has the power to summon forth spiritual reflection, serves in this narrative as an inspiration for a final rumination. In pausing to look back upon what has been written herein up to this point, I recognize that the ruminations about to be reported in this final part of the narrative represent a sharp change from what has gone before in this book. If, as was mentioned in the introduction, the Neumann shrine is worthy of a pilgrimage, perhaps undertaking a departure from sauntering along the weatherworn streets of Kensington in order to engage in reflections that the shrine can elicit will not be deemed out of place.

The ruminations that follow will attempt to put into perspective the two tokens of distinction associated with Neumann—his sainthood, and his philosophy of Christian formation. The latter may be considered as being embodied in the parochial school system of which he was the pioneering architect, and which impacted all those shaped by a parochial school education. How well has that system equipped its graduates (like myself and many others whose religious formation was experienced at schools like the Ascension), to contend with the challenges of the 20th century and beyond? But first, some consideration will be given to Neumann from the perspective of him having been declared a saint and a model for Christian living.

When the proposal was first voiced that Neumann be placed on track to be declared a saint, some wondered whether Neumann had manifested anything "heroic." Traditional hagiography in the Church gives prominence to heroic exploits and miraculous incidents in the holy lives of those whom it heralds as saints. Dying for the faith, performing miracles, displaying behaviors that defy the laws of nature, or undergoing the harshest of rigors in locales plagued by disease and destitution—such are the kinds of features often associated with a saintly life. The martyrs of the early Church went to their deaths rather than renounce their faith. Joan of Arc led armies, and if she is not technically considered a martyr, her compliance with the angels' voices ultimately led to her execution. Oscar Romero spoke out against injustice and paid the price with his life. Damien de Veuster served the community of lepers on the island of Molokai and became terminally ill from leprosy himself. Theresa of Calcutta served the sick and dying in the blighted streets of Calcutta. Joseph of Cupertino, reportedly, tended to levitate while at prayer and often had to be restrained by the ankles by his confreres lest he smash his head on the chapel ceiling.

Saints tended to be depicted as so much larger than life as to be far beyond serving as models for imitation. Rather, they serve to inspire awe. The life of Neumann, on the other hand, suggested little of the spectacularly heroic or the sensationally miraculous. He did not claim to see visions. Neumann gave no evidence of having experiences that violated natural laws. He did not die a martyr's death, although he practiced a lifestyle afflicted by stress and showed a predilection for physical austerities.

In a homily presented on the 200th anniversary of his birth at Saint Alphonsus Church in Baltimore, his sanctity was characterized with the words: "He did ordinary things in an extraordinary way." The statement evokes the words of two other saints— those of Saint Jane de Chantal and Theresa of Calcutta— whereby it is asserted that we cannot always offer God great things, but at each instant we can do little things with great love. What was being suggested is that sainthood is not restricted to those models of holiness of yore, to those saints whose herculean feats of sanctity rather precluded them from being objects of imitation. The consequence of placing sainthood within reach of all believers is, of course, that then no one can claim disqualification for such status by virtue of being less than superhuman. At any rate, if Neumann cannot be dismissed as being beatifically beyond the pale but is nevertheless a saint, upon what is his sainthood based?

Neumann's interior life would likely contain clues as to what precisely comprised his spirituality. But Neumann was notably not given to self-promotion or to advertising his sentiments, so how to obtain insight into his spirituality?

It turns out that Neumann bequeathed to posterity two testaments. One is a brief, hastily-written autobiography which he composed under orders upon being named bishop of Philadelphia.[52] The other is Neumann's spiritual journal which he kept while a theology student at the University of Prague.[53] The journal was unearthed after his death by his nephew, John Berger, and was not intended for publication.

The autobiography paints a rather idyllic picture of Neumann's upbringing in Prachatitz, Bohemia, and of the time he spent at the seminary in Budweis, where he excelled academically and enjoyed a supportive network of friends. While in Budweis, he applied for and received one of the few scholarships to complete his theological studies at the prestigious and selective University of Prague. He was motivated to study in Prague not so that he could lay claim to the distinction of studying at an illustrious university, but because he would have the opportunity to study English and French. He felt that those two languages would be indispensable for his future missionary work in the New World. When he arrived in Prague, he was disappointed to find that those language classes were closed to seminary students. On top of that blow, he was not able to obtain much satisfaction in his theology classes. He felt that the professors were too liberal for his taste. As he notes in the autobiography: "It cost me a great deal of effort and self-conquest to study subjects and opinions, the foolishness of which I had already learned to see through."[54]

Such a sentiment evokes the memory of another alumnus of the University of Prague. Four centuries earlier, the reformer, John Hus, expressed disapproval of what he regarded as the excessive sophistication of theology completely removed from the pastoral mission of the clergy. Neumann stayed the course in spite of these reversals and passed, though his grades slipped. But then there turned out to be one final stroke of bad luck, when he learned that ordinations would be postponed at the time of his graduation, owing to a surplus of priests in the diocese. Neumann rounds out his autobiography with a brief description of his voyage to America and his good fortune at finding Bishop Dubois of New York, who ordained him and assigned him to pastoral work.

When it comes to Neumann's journal, the tone of discourse is markedly different. In these pages, written by the young theology student, an intense spiritual struggle is revealed which belies Neumann's storied reserved exterior. As a theology student at a prestigious school, he found himself no longer enfolded in the small-town warmth of Budweis, where he could count on support and benevolence. The cosmopolitan city of Prague—full of sophistication and of historical significance—was unforgivingly indifferent to whatever guileless newcomer showed up from the provinces. One may be blessed by being raised in a loving family and being educated in a supportive environment when young. There will, however, inevitably come a time when one encounters others who are impervious to, or even hostile to, one's existence. In Prague, Neumann found himself in an environment largely indifferent to him and was abruptly thrown back upon his spiritual resources.

Neumann's entries in his journal show that the achievement of self-confidence did not come easily to him at the University of Prague. Some journal entries present Neumann's painful fear that he was disliked by many: "The bitterness and chagrin I experience from the Prefect's [a kind of administrative dean] dislike and disregard make me fear that my pride is emerging again."

In another entry, he again complains: "The President and all good people despise me . . . Jesus, my uncertain relation towards the President cause me great anxiety . . . my aversion for the President increases . . . If I sometimes seek his company, he avoids me, he seems to despise me."

Nor did he receive much solicitude from his peers, who apparently viewed him as rigidly orthodox and punctilious, as he notes on December 10th, 1834: "Boehm received a letter from Müller at Leitmerz in which the latter scoffs at my exaggerated orthodoxy and tries to get Nowack to take sides against me. They read my letter in the study hall and my feelings were hurt."

From these entries, it is clear that his sense of isolation was reaching a crisis point, but he was able to incorporate his pain into his prayer life: "Dear God, everybody is displeased with me.

How can I evoke their affections? I am so fainthearted and timid! Thinking about my friends today made me feel so disconsolate, especially after supper, that I started to cry! Here I am, with all my carelessness and indifference, while my friends in Budweis are surrounded by remarkable people and enjoy wise and holy spiritual direction! They don't even think of me anymore. In my loneliness and grief they have forgotten all about me."

Just how seriously Neumann teetered on the edge of an emotional crisis can be seen in the following entry: "My God, do not let the despair of mine continue . . . it could lead to suicide." But Neumann was up to the challenge, largely by giving expression to his distress in his prayer life and locating the problem in his pride. Neumann was not one of those supremely confident people for whom the cultivation of humility is of negligible utility. He realized that the only way he could mitigate the pain brought on by his hypersensitivity was through sharing his pain with God in prayer and through praying for the virtue of humility.

In an otherwise quotidian incident, recounted in a journal entry of October 11, 1834, Neumann's pride was brought to his attention acutely. While on a trip into town, he had purchased a bag of plums. Upon entering the seminary campus, he encountered the school president. This is the very president with whom he had a relationship fraught with vexation.

"Are you planning to eat all those plums yourself?" inquired the president, probably in a spirit of light-hearted repartee.

"Of course not," replied Neumann. "I plan to share them with my classmates."

As Neumann continued on his way, he was overcome with shame, he confessed, as he had no such plan.

Apparently Neumann's two years of study at the University of Prague transpired without him being assigned a spiritual director, an omission for which Neumann offers no explanation. It is imaginable that he simply lacked the inclination to bring a lot of attention to himself. At any rate, perhaps he was motivated to keep a spiritual journal to serve as a substitute for his lack of guidance, as he notes, "O Jesus, thou knowest my sad condition! Here I am without a guide, without an advisor. Lord, teach me how to pray, that I may obtain what is so necessary for me!"

What is most noteworthy about Neumann keeping a spiritual journal is his recognition that he had spiritual work to do. The journal represents Neumann's ongoing examination of conscience. The persistence with which he carried out this exercise manifests a significant amount of character. Neumann recognized the enemy within, that is, his own inclination to be governed by self-indulgence. He perceived within himself a distressing disposition towards pride, sloth, envy, mendacity, tepidity, and a lukewarm regard to his attendance at Mass and in other devotional exercises. He complains as well about his tendency to be beset by temptations against the virtue of purity. "I am indeed a sinner and yet I want to be perfect," he recounts in an entry on February 15, 1835. He goes on, relentlessly: "My Lord Jesus, behold me, defiled by sin! Again I have stained the holy garment of purity which Thy Blood has so often cleaned. O Father, hear my prayer! Give me the true spirit of penance, that, through the humble supplications of my contrite heart, I may again receive pardon. Since my last confession, O my Jesus, I have fallen more frequently than usual! My incessant combats, my unholy desires, my tepidity and discouragement, have made me forget many great sins." Later on March 6, 1835, he adds: "Thoughts against purity cause me considerable pain; however, God has been gracious enough to help me." In his determination to lead a Godward life, his awareness of his sinfulness liberated him from leading a life ruled by his concupiscent appetites.

The spiritual work that Neumann did during his years in Prague, as reflected in his journal, certainly bore much fruit, as evidenced in the pastoral duties that he discharged during his time spent as priest and bishop. If the Battle of Waterloo was won on the fields of Eton, as the British say, what Neumann accomplished as bishop was made possible, arguably, by the spiritual work that he sustained during his formative years when he was a university student. His approach to the spiritual life was born out of the experience of much inner discord. If Neumann was indifferent to self-promotion, it was because he was at war with his ego. He was determined not to be ruled by those inclinations which conspired to subvert his spiritual progress. As his nephew, John Berger reports: one of his most prized possessions when he embarked for America was a copy of Lorenzo Scupoli's 1589 spiritual classic, *The Spiritual Combat*. It was that image of an interior battle—a battle against the egoistic passions that draw one away from God—that characterized Neumann's interior life. In terms of William James's binary classification of religious believers into "healthy-minded souls" and "sick souls,"[55] Neumann would seem to belong decidedly to the latter. Neuman saw himself as being defective, beset by unholy inclinations that drew him away from God and that required a strict discipline consisting of continual prayer, reception of the sacrament of Penance, and acts of self-denial. If he saw himself as damaged, as afflicted with unholy impulses and inclinations, he committed himself to his faith in Christ as the means to gain salvation.

Like all people, Neumann experienced his share of internal conflict, but he was determined to be guided by his religious faith in dealing with whatever conflicts that he was challenged with. His journal presents the internal drama of his war with concupiscence--the fateful legacy of original sin, as traditional theology taught. While it is difficult to know exactly what constituted Neumann's experience of concupiscence, that is to say, his experience of inordinate desire, it is clear from his journal that the war was waged without quarter. It can be deduced from the journal that Neumann considered himself to be in some way flawed and beset by impulses that could not be reconciled with his spiritual goals. It was his objective, in the spiritual work that he undertook, to center his life not on self-indulgence and self-aggrandizement, but on Christ and his commission to his followers to dedicate their lives to serving others.

Perhaps it was Neumann's consciousness of a region of darkness in his soul that afflicted him with what may be regarded today as deficits in self-esteem. His hypersensitivity and shyness can be seen as deriving from his ongoing struggle to combat drives that could have taken over the direction of his life and moved him away from the Godward life that was his prevailing desire. Perhaps those drives at times contributed to feelings of self-disgust. When in his journal Neumann complains about his shortcomings, a tendency towards hyperscrupulosity is put on display, and the faults which he catalogues can seem petty and banal. Or are they really? The offenses which vexed Neumann were decidedly victimless ones. When he reproached himself for impulses driven by pride, or for feelings of envy, or for distractedness while at devotional exercises, or for indulgence in erotic thoughts, he is occupying himself strictly with his interior dispositions. Neumann was determined to bring his interior dispositions in conformity with the mind of Christ. One's heart represents the zone where spiritual work is carried out. While it is true that emotional impulses arise involuntarily, the cultivation of such feelings, which are largely inspired by the pleasure principle, serves to allow bad habits to take root.

Neumann recognized this, and by remaining faithful to the promises of the Gospels he gave testimony to the strength and to the healing power that the Gospels possess. His strength of character is indicated in his determination to reach his spiritual goals in spite of whatever psychological shortcomings he suffered from. Many who are models of good psychological adjustment and emotional wellness have not accomplished what Neumann was able to accomplish. Without his heroic determination to lead a Godward life it is difficult to know what would have happened to him.

It could have been a consequence of his rigorous program of self-discipline for him to have cultivated a rather judgmental and pompous pastoral style, along the lines of which may be described as the Jansenistic attitude.

Cornelius Jansen, a Dutch theologian, writing in the 17th century when theological speculation generated impassioned controversy, described human nature as being hopelessly degraded by original sin and a God who, by virtue of some unfathomable design, bestows favor on only a small, ostensibly dutiful cohort of Christian believers. Despite much of his theology being condemned as heretical, Jansen's thought enjoyed great cachet and the somber cast of his theology permeated much of Catholic practice in the ensuing several centuries. This theology likely accounts for the austere and severely penitential orientation of Neumann's spirituality. It was an approach to the spiritual life which Neumann could have represented in his pastoral work as the standard for salvation that sets one apart from the multitude of lost souls, and for which only a select few are qualified to meet. But his was not a one-size-fits-all spirituality. He knew, and fought for, what *he* had to do to achieve *his* goal. He knew what *his* uniquely personal challenges consisted of, and he recognized that his spiritual trials would be with him throughout his life. Others, those whom he served as pastor, would have their own unique challenges and would adopt that spirituality suited to their particular circumstances and personality. Neumann was not constituted to regard himself as being a better Christian than others. In the light of his rather self-abasing personality, it cannot be imagined that he conceived of himself as a saint, nor that he took for granted the salvation of his soul. In addition to that, even if there was often a gloomy, Jansenist cast to his guilt-ridden and very scrupulous conscience, his spirituality was distinguished, as indicated in his journal, by a very personal relationship with Christ. For him, God was not some distant, inscrutable being, rather, God was manifested to him through the human face of Christ. It was that experience of a close relationship with Christ that constituted the center of his spiritual life. It was his commitment to striving after an imitation of Christ that permitted a sublimation of the drives which did not serve his spiritual aspirations.

Neumann was unlikely to have been surprised that he had to deal with significant challenges in his years as Philadelphia's bishop. His grip on reality being solid, he was surely aware that he was a disappointment as a bishop—a disappointment to many of the priests of the diocese, to many of his fellow American bishops, as well as to much of the upper crust of Philadelphia society. He likely concurred with their assessment that he was unsuited for the office of bishop;

However, Neumann's self-assessment was not a particularly dependable one in the light of his accomplishments. The painful experiences that comprised his time as bishop served to inspire Neumann to enter more closely into union with Christ's own suffering. Christ himself, as recounted in the Gospels, had to contend with a considerable amount of opposition from and disapproval by those who held positions of power in Judea—opposition and disapproval which ultimately led to his execution. There was profound disappointment among his followers attendant upon the tragic outcome of Christ's life of service to others. As one of the disciples on the road to Emmaus lamented: "We had hoped that he was the one who was going to redeem Israel." (Luke 24:21)

The hopes and dreams swirling around Judea at the time of a glorious Messiah were shattered as a result of the spectacle of Christ's ignominious and agonizing death—a death which featured torture, then crucifixion between two common criminals. Thus was dealt a serious blow to the grandiose theology—a theology featuring an omnipotent God and a hoped-for majestic Messiah—that represented the longings of the earnest adherents of the theistic traditions embodied in the Old Testament. Certainly the portrait of a suffering Messiah bent on serving others rather than smiting Judea's enemies, was foreshadowed in the Old Testament, as in the words of the prophets. The message was not received, and perhaps is not received, without an element of spiritual struggle. Neumann can be celebrated as one whose spiritual struggle enabled him to understand that God's power is manifested in love, energizing him to spend his life manifesting God's love to those who often counted least in the eyes of the world.

Arguably the Biblical text which lay at the foundation of Neumann's spirituality was Philippians Chapter 2 (Vs. 5–8): "In your relationships with one another, have the same mindset as Christ Jesus: Who, being God in his very nature, did not consider equality with God something to be used to his own advantage; rather, he made himself nothing by taking the very nature of a servant, being made in human likeness. As being found in appearance as a man, he humbled himself by becoming obedient to death—even death on a cross!" The Christian life involves a reordering of the meaning of power. If Neumann failed to impress by virtue of a less than commanding self-representation, his spirituality, founded upon the Philippians' verse, had fruitful effect.

CHAPTER 14

THE PAROCHIAL SCHOOL SYSTEM

Neumann's Legacy and the Consequences

The purpose of this reflection is to weigh what the consequences are of being inducted, as a youth educated in an elementary school like Kensington's Ascension, into a decisively monistic, dogmatically-based belief system. When Neumann assumed his post as bishop of Philadelphia in 1852, the Nativist riots in Kensington had taken place a mere eight years earlier. Since that time, Know-Nothing political parties scored a significant number of electoral victories in the local scene. The climate of hostility towards Catholics, particularly those recent arrivals from Ireland, had scarcely abated. The Catholic hierarchies' determination to fashion an educational system specifically geared to the beleaguered Catholic community had a rather isolative consequence to that community. That is to say, the parochial school system, having been launched at the height of the period of Nativist hostility towards Catholic immigrants, settled itself into a rather defensive posture that characterized the system well into the twentieth century.

Generations of school children—descendants of those 19th-century, rather destitute immigrants who populated Kensington—were recipients of the claim that the repository of truth is to be found in the magisterium of the Catholic Church.

The countless credos represented in the plurality of perspectives on view around the world were characterized as being fragmentary in their grip on truth, at best, or as being manifestly mired in error, at worst. It is needless to say that the cognitive reach of young minds is bound by age-appropriate limitations. In that light, rather than directing commentary to the pedagogic strategy employed at the Ascension, it is the objective here to consider how such a dogmatic vision fares when those shaped by the religious formation of the educational system launched by Neumann undergo further cognitive development in the post-Vatican II world. This rumination, therefore, departs from presenting a record of historical events, whether such events have taken place within living memory or unfolded in a barely remembered distant past. The focus is, instead, on a culture shaped by an educational system that was very defensive in its stance toward the world external to it.

In addition, this reflection aspires to address the challenges faced by those shaped by a parochial school education, such as that offered by the Ascension or at high schools such as Northeast Catholic. What happens to graduates of that system when they move on to higher education where, often, the measure of truth was held to be found in empirical method rather than in metaphysical or theological systems? Will the religious sensibility shaped by a parochial school education survive the college classroom?

Arguably, the signature achievement of Neumann as bishop was his expansion of the parochial school system. In spite of his rather characteristic lament on the eve of his consecration as bishop, that he would rather be led to the gallows than become bishop of Philadelphia, he made use of the opportunity to contribute some benefit to the diocese, however much he regarded the office as an uncoveted one. He put tireless effort into building schools. While there were two parochial schools in the diocese in 1852 when he took office, in 1860 there were over ninety.

Pastoral solicitude was his guiding principle. For generations of children of the diocese, the Christian formation practiced in the parochial school system would be governed by a spirit of solicitude--a solicitude which sought to ensure protection from a frequently hostile world.

At the beginning, that meant providing a Catholic education to the children of poor, but hardworking immigrant families like those in Kensington, in a setting hermetically shielded from the nativist, anti-Catholic animus prevalent at that historical moment. But it also meant protecting Catholic children from assaults, not only against Catholicism but against religion in general, which were intensifying during the nineteenth century and thereafter, in the intellectual arena. Undeniably, it may be said that the Catholic culture which took shape in the mid-nineteenth century and which became a feature of that culture as a result of the religious formation carried out in the Catholic schools was decidedly defensive—that of a culture under siege.

As one of the pioneering architects of the parochial school system in Philadelphia, Neumann was instrumental in crafting the guiding principles underlying the religious formation conducted in the schools. Basically, it was deemed necessary to shield parochial school students from all external threats to the faith. Secular learning was cast as a serious threat to the kind of "simple" faith that Neumann espoused, and as something that must be avoided. That also meant promoting an apologetic which asserted that the Catholic expression of Christianity represented the one true Church and therefore is the ultimate arbiter of religious truth—the Church founded by Christ Himself, however many denominational variations of Christianity have arisen since Luther launched the Reformation. The world may present a plurality of perspectives in regard to questions addressing the meaning of existence, but in the parochial school classroom, the deposit of truth was located in the Catholic Church. Consequently, there was a palpably hermetic character to religious instruction in the parochial school classroom. Such a strategy of throwing up defensive bulwarks against external threats worked well as long as the course of life of those educated in parochial schools like those in a working-class neighborhood Kensington followed a predictable pattern within a confined setting. That pattern initially was characterized by eight grades of elementary education followed by, as far as Kensington was concerned, a job in a textile mill for men, or life as a housewife for women.

Kensington became the prototypical blue collar, working class neighborhood, and if the condition of life in Kensington was rather unpoetic and a monotonous job in a textile mill lacked glamor, it nevertheless provided a relatively stable income. That is to say, few Kensington families accumulated great wealth, and entering the workforce once one was able in order to earn money took precedence over the luxury of pursuing more education beyond elementary school.

When the high school became a feature of mass education in the 20th century, the Archdiocese of Philadelphia kept pace with the expectations of the faithful by constructing ample and tuition-free educational facilities that offered grades nine through twelve. The defensive spirit that characterized religious formation in the elementary school classroom continued relatively unchanged. That is to say, the Catholic culture as experienced in a neighborhood like Kensington was represented as being under siege and needed to be cultivated in relative isolation from the surrounding environment.

The character of religious formation in the system launched by Neumann certainly reflected Neumann's distrust of "worldliness." For Neumann, the desire to be "worldly" is nothing more than a fascination with the seductiveness of sin and a desire to yield to impulses that promise some as yet unknown pleasure. The drama manifested in Neumann's journal is precisely a form of combat waged by Neumann against the dangers posed by the "world" that places the soul in jeopardy. Perhaps the danger represented to the soul by the "world" is best expressed in a sermon of John Henry Newman: "One of the chief causes of the wickedness which is everywhere seen in the world, and in which, alas! each of us has more or less a share, is our curiosity to have some fellowship with darkness, some experience of sin, to know what the pleasures of sin are like. I believe it is often thought unmanly by many persons (though they may not like to say so in plain words) and a thing to be ashamed of, to have no knowledge of sin by experience, as if it augured a strange seclusion from the world, a childish ignorance of life, a simpleness and narrowness of mind, and a superstitious, slavish fear. Not to know sin by experience brings upon a man the laughter and jests of his companions."[56]

It was precisely this human inclination to taste the pleasures that the world has to offer which Neumann felt would divert him from centering his life on Christ. If that meant being perceived as prudish, then so be it. As he recorded in his journal which he began writing while studying at the University of Prague, Neumann was the butt of jokes due to his hypersensitivity and, likely, his unworldliness. It is inconceivable, however, that he was unaware of the human drive to fill the experience of emptiness by seeking sexual adventure or by turning to the euphoria or self-forgetfulness that consciousness-altering substances can deliver. In Neumann, that emptiness would be filled by his faith.

In the face of the ridicule directed towards him while in Prague, he resisted the temptation to give in to pride and endured the derision as his cross to bear. "Worldliness," therefore, was not a condition of life consistent with his understanding of Christian formation, and it might be said it was a characteristic of Catholic school education in Philadelphia that "secular" learning was looked upon with distrust.

More serious challenges to religious faith would present themselves as educational aspirations continued to rise. Being content with a high school education for their children would not do for the 20th century descendants of those early immigrant families. By the midpoint of the 20th century, many of the descendants of those humble 19th century immigrant families began to expect more education for their children than just a secondary school education. The dream of a better life would materialize, it was hoped, by virtue of a college diploma, creating the opportunity to rise from the ranks of the working class to the professional class. Needless to say, attendance at a university would challenge those products of the parochial school system with a full range of opinions and conjectures which did not always put the Church or religion in a favorable light. Exposure to what Neumann referred to as the "labored investigations" of atheistic or agnostic academicians, which could be minimized in the parochial school system, would be inevitable at the university level. The "ism's" such as atheism and skepticism, among others, from which the church hierarchy sought to shield the products of a parochial school education enjoy great cache in the halls of higher education.

Prominent among those "ism's" are secularism, atheism, and skepticism. The first of those, *secularism*, which is derived from the Latin word for "the ages," and by implication, the "world," holds great appeal to youth on the threshold of adulthood. After all, for many, being "unworldly"—a quality which characterized Neumann's spirituality—is not an attractive condition of life. The next, *atheism,* is obviously antagonistic to religious faith. But it is the third "ism," *skepticism,* which tends to enfold the impressionable college student in its spiritless embrace most enduringly. Neither theistic nor atheistic, skepticism offers no vision except to countenance a life lacking any self-transcendence. Pontius Pilate, the Roman governor of Judea when Jesus was brought to trial, submitted himself as the great avatar of skepticism. When, in answer to Jesus's assertion that He was sent into the world to testify to the Truth (John 18:37), Pilate shot back cynically: "What is truth?" (John 18:38). Undoubtedly, Pilate's rhetorical question warms the hearts of all the world's proponents of hardheaded skepticism.

How can faith be preserved in a milieu in which an antireligious project is in full swing? The two elements deemed essential for Christian formation as a means to preserve faith were a "simple faith" and protection from exposure to antireligious viewpoints. There was an occasion during Neumann's episcopate when Neumann indicated his preference for what he called a "simple faith." As recounted by Curley in his biography of Neumann,[57] the bishop was asked to offer his opinion about the recent publication of Darwin's theory of evolution which was throwing into question the truth of the biblical account of creation contained in the book of Genesis. The effect of Darwin's *The Origin of Species* was to unsettle the faith of many, not only at that time, but has continued to provoke crises of faith ever since. Replied Neumann, as quoted by Curley: "the simple faith in the opening pages of the Bible would do a man more good than the labored investigations of agnostic or atheistic scientists." Neumann likely felt little concern for the prescientific cosmology contained in the Genesis account of creation, but valued the text for the theological doctrine contained therein—that the material world and everything in it is created by a Supreme Being who remains in close relationship with that creation. The "simple faith" of presumably unsophisticated believers need to be protected from the "scientific investigations" of those investigators who factor out all matters related to the role of a Creator, notwithstanding the compelling evidence which controverts the literal account of creation presented in the book of Genesis. Furthermore, if the truth of Genesis cannot be counted on, what about other biblical texts? It would seem that a more skeptical approach to biblical texts is warranted.

The nature of skepticism merits further examination but a few brief words about the Church's efforts to combat the modern world's secularistic and otherwise "modernist" assaults against religious faith. The religious formation carried out in a parochial school like the Ascension in Kensington—part of the educational system of which Neumann was a pioneering architect—was designed to preserve what may be termed Neumann's "simple faith." During Neumann's time the effort to achieve that objective was conducted in a social environment unfriendly to newly-arrived Catholic immigrants, who were perceived by the native-born to be upsetting the traditional demographic of the country. Along with protecting Catholic schoolchildren from what was regarded by the Catholic hierarchy as Protestant propaganda, protection was also deemed necessary from assaults originating from the intellectual field which were inimical to religious faith. Neumann's approach to Christian formation was congruent with the attempts of the Church's magisterium to conduct a fiercely-fought campaign to combat what was regarded as heretical notions associated with the secularistic thought of the Enlightenment. Measures adopted by the Church included the issuance of a series of papal encyclicals which enumerated dozens of modern "errors," such as rationalism, communism, relativism, skepticism, and others. A document known as the "Syllabus of Errors" was issued by Pius ix in 1864 which provided a list of about eighty "-isms" which merited condemnation. Significant expansion of the Index of Forbidden Books was carried out, on which was included a variety of the philosophical works, such as those of Descartes, Kant, Rousseau, Voltaire and others. Fictional works of the nineteenth century were not excluded, and French novelists such as Balzac, Zola, Stendhal, and Dumas came under censure. The purpose of the Index was not simply to warn away believers from reading them but to declare such works to be occasions of sin, whether novelistic plots featured licentious lifestyles or whether works of philosophy featured philosophical arguments at variance to Church teaching—arguments which presumably to those whose faith was fragile might possess a seductive attractiveness. These efforts to counter those trends put in motion by the secular values of the Enlightenment culminated in the Papal declaration of infallibility in 1870—a declaration which roughly coincided with the absorption of the Papal States into the Republic of Italy.

If we may characterize the products of Kensington's parochial schools, such as the Ascension, as Neumann's spiritual descendants, how would these heirs of a "simple faith," nurtured in a protective cocoon sometimes characterized as a Catholic ghetto, negotiate the halls of academia where skepticism enjoys great currency? But what exactly is the nature of that skepticism? While skepticism has existed as long as philosophers have conducted inquiries into the nature of knowledge, modern skepticism can be traced back to the seventeenth century, when the French philosopher René Descartes embarked upon his quest to identify a method which would yield reliable, or preferably, certain knowledge. Descartes undertook his philosophical investigations by throwing into question the capability of the mind to apprehend what is real and true. He resolved to begin by taking nothing on faith. He went further. Warming up to his determination to identify all the possible ways whereby our knowledge rests on shaky foundations, Descartes imagined the possible existence of a "malicious demon"—a powerful trickster who has constructed an illusory world, that is, the external world perceived by our senses that we are deceived into believing really exists. While he endowed the condition of radical doubt with respectability, he ultimately identified one elemental reality which he felt was undeniably real—his own thinking mind ("cogito, ergo sum"). It is not the objective here to trace the trajectory of Descartes' course of thought. Suffice it to say that he launched an ongoing reassessment by modern philosophers of the validity of what human beings claim to know. The branch of philosophy known as epistemology being given center stage, a variety of conclusions was drawn, among which has been the glorification of empirical method as being the surest, nay, for some, the only, formula for arriving at certain knowledge. That is to say, an assertion may be regarded as true insofar as it is determinable in accordance with the standards set by empirical method. Modern life is the beneficiary of the significant progress made in bringing to light the scientific laws which govern the natural world. This progress has been brought about by the painstaking labors of dedicated scientists who have subjected themselves—ideally—to the rigorous procedures which govern empirical investigation. Thus has there been dramatic progress in advancing human understanding in the fields of biology, physics, and chemistry, bringing about significant improvement in the quality of modern life, at least in the first world. At the same time, these impressive achievements of modern science have, to some extent, eroded the prestige of metaphysical and theological speculation. If theology was, in the Middle Ages, the queen of the sciences, the category, "science," in the modern world, is circumscribed in its explorations insofar as it seeks to uncover truths in the only world that it regards as "real," namely, the natural world. Within the purview of modern science, there is no "supernatural" world. Hypotheses which cannot be operationalized for empirical investigation are regarded as being devoid of meaning. Thus, in the opinion of one evolutionary biologist, Richard Dawkins, religious believers are afflicted with delusional thinking, because, to his mind, they give assent to claims for which there is no evidence. The title of his book, *The God Delusion*, says it all.

In the face of the claim that religious beliefs have reference to nothing that is demonstrably provable, the concession may be put forth that indeed religious beliefs are not founded upon evidence that can be assembled in strict accordance to the methodology prescribed by empirical science under laboratory conditions. But such a concession does not mean that religious claims rest upon no evidence at all. Giving assent to claims for which there exists no evidence is nonsensical. If the empirical scientist studies the world of nature in order to bring to light its laws, the human desire to question and to know concerns itself with questions relating to existence itself. That is to say, the empirical scientist is occupied with problems to be solved, while the questions posed in the sphere of religion revolve around life's mysteries. There are those who deny the existence of God and there are those who report indifference to the question of God's existence. But the datum of experience which is undeniable is that human beings do not generate their own being. Upon that fact rests the human aspiration for connection with the ground of being. "As soon as we become fully aware of our own existence, as soon as we grasp the reality of the world around us and of contingent being, we find ourselves face to face with the question of a Pure and Absolute Being, necessarily implied by the presence of our own relative and contingent existence."[58]

The experience of human wonder, generating existential questions such as, why do we exist?, or, how did the material world come into being?, is universal, even if some scientific fundamentalists dismiss such questions of an existential nature as meaningless. On the other hand, the findings of science which have impacted modern life rest upon work generally performed by specialists. We depend upon specialists to understand how natural phenomena work, whether it is a matter of computer technology, aviation, medical technology, biochemistry, and the like. We deem it not necessary that the lay person possess an understanding of the technical aspects of contemporary scientific know-how. That type of knowledge need not be appropriated by the average person, or the non-specialist. On the other hand, questions related to the nature of existence itself, such as the purpose or value thereof, are questions touching every person. A rocket scientist is respected for having expertise that most people do not have, but everyone feels that he or she has the right to an opinion about religion. Those "opinions" stem from a person's orientation to those fundamental questions about life's meaning, whether a person views life as a God-given gift which is to be reverently cared for, or whether life is viewed nihilistically as being without purpose or value.

It is worth putting into perspective just what the significance of scientific knowledge is, that is, knowledge about the laws of nature wrought by dedicated scientists. The acquisition of such knowledge and the consequent improvements brought about in medical care and communications which have characterized the modern world can be a source of pride—pride about the impressive capacity of the human mind to penetrate nature's secrets. Such a capability on the part of the human mind can served to arouse an inflated estimation of the potential of the human intellect—what might be termed a "God complex." It was the human desire "to be like God" that made Adam and Eve susceptible to the seductive words of the serpent in the Garden of Eden: "when you eat of it (the forbidden fruit) your eyes will be opened, and you will be like God" (Genesis 3:5). That forgetfulness of creaturehood represents the essence of original sin, and accounts for the manifold ills that have beset humanity, at least as is asserted in the biblical text. If human beings have a fateful tendency to forget their status as creatures—after all, we do not generate our own being but are entrusted with it by who-knows-what—it is well to remember that the knowledge wrought by scientific investigation is not benign. The image of the power-obsessed "mad scientist" has been endlessly exploited in novels and films in which apocalyptic scenarios unfold as an experiment slips out of control, such as in Mary Shelley's *Frankenstein*, Michael Crichton's *Jurassic Park*, or H. G. Wells' *The Island of Doctor Moreau*, to mention just a few.

Aside from scientific experiments run amok which have supplied the entertainment world with stories featuring horrifying scenarios, perhaps a more frightening sequel to scientific discoveries is their application to the development of ever more lethal weaponry. The sustained rapid-fire capability of the machine gun, the use of which mowed down tens of thousands of British infantrymen on the first day of the Battle of the Somme in 1916, suggested to many at the time that the ultimate doomsday weapon had made its appearance. Later, it was not long after the structure of the atom was brought to light that the production of nuclear weapons ushered in a new era of unprecedented lethal weaponry. In recent years, drone technology has made it possible to deliver lethal destruction with pinpoint accuracy from stratospheric heights, while the agent of the mayhem sits before a computer console while sipping coffee in an air-conditioned room far from any field of battle. This escalating development of ever more lethal weaponry has to do with what Jonathan Schell calls "the path of science." That is to say, "while science is without doubt the most powerful revolutionary force in the world, no one directs that force. For science is a process of submission, in which the mind does not dictate to nature but seeks out and then bows to nature's laws, letting its conclusions be guided by that which *is,* independent of our will. From the political point of view, therefore, scientific findings, some lending themselves to evil, some to good, and some to both, simply pour forth from the laboratory in senseless profusion, offering the world now a neutron bomb, now bacteria that devour oil, now a vaccine to prevent polio, now a cloned frog."[59] Human beings being constituted both by will as well as by intellect, it is human choice which confronts whatever discoveries about nature's laws that human ingenuity has uncovered. Thus do, in the words of Schell, "mankind's own judgments, moods, and decisions loom up with an unlooked-for, terrifying importance." It is frightening to try to imagine what may lay in store for future generations as scientific discoveries continue to unfold. What new weapons of mass destruction, and new weapon delivery systems, can be expected in the future of humankind?

    If scientists confine their investigations to that world which represents for them the only "knowable" world, namely, the world of the measurable as discerned in nature, their quest for certain, empirically-verifiable knowledge finds a counterpart among many religious believers. That is to say, some religious believers, not to be outdone by the supreme confidence which scientists demonstrate regarding the truth of their scientific findings, triumphantly employ the language of certainty in the characterization of their beliefs. The two camps—religious fundamentalists, and those who might be termed scientific fundamentalists—share a fixation about certainty. It may be said that both camps fail to make a distinction between two levels of knowledge—one level which occupies itself with the material world of nature, and one which addresses the world of meaning and value. The scientific fundamentalist truncates human experience by denying reality to whatever is not measurable empirically under laboratory conditions, while the religious fundamentalist attempts to formulate statements of religious belief as if they were demonstrable conclusions to empirical investigation. But statements of religious belief have not been appropriated as the result of empirical investigation carried out in the laboratory. They nonetheless stem from experience, and the foundational experiences that characterize Christianity are recorded in the four Gospels. In those four texts is laid out the transformation that the followers of Christ underwent by virtue of their witnessing of Christ's life and death, of his ministry to others and his acceptance of the dire consequences attendant upon the opposition to his ministry by those in power. The Apostles' experience of the Risen Christ illuminated for them the nature of the mystery of God—that God's power resides in love, that by loving others we share in God's own life, and that by sharing in God's life victory over death is won. In their experience Christ is the very incarnation of God. The proclamation by the Apostles of Christ's divinity came about as the result of a long process. The learning curve undergone by them reached its culmination in their encounters with the Risen

Christ. It is such religious experience that bequeaths knowledge implicated in making decisions and performing judgments, and it is those activities that constitute the grist of everyone's life, whether religious believers or religious skeptics.

A higher education may conspire to unsettle religious faith by devalorizing religious knowledge and promoting skepticism, but the reason for this is not chiefly the trenchant commentary contained in the writings of anti-religious commentators like Dawkins. The significant factor is the failure of religious believers like Christians to put into practice their beliefs so that the face of Christ may be manifested to the world. Christians—of whatever denomination—often get caught up with representing their "faith" as a set of propositions that have the same kind of objective reality as scientific findings. But religious faith is constituted by a kind of knowledge which can only be established and validated by virtue of that faith being lived out in the world. Conceiving religious faith as primarily a matter of the mental acceptance of a set of propositions about what are in effect mysteries distorts the meaning of religious faith and creates inhospitable divisions among people. The binary division in question sets those who claim to have the right answers against those, in the mind of the religious fundamentalist, who do not have the right answer and are living in darkness. Prominent in that camp is the personality type consisting of those who have a compulsive need to feel in possession of the correct answers to all questions relating to life's mysteries. But do the Gospels really support an understanding of religious faith as being a matter of being in possession of and holding forth on answers to questions? Life may be characterized as a test, but not a test in the shape of a scholastic exam soliciting answers to a series of exam questions. Christian faith is tested by how well the Christian believer treats those who, in the eyes of society, do not count. "Go, and do likewise," Jesus charges his followers upon recounting the parable of the Good Samaritan. Throughout the Gospels Jesus shows care for society's outcastes—lepers, tax collectors, foreigners, beggars, prostitutes, and migrants. Chapter 25 of Matthew's Gospel spells out how faith is tested: "Inasmuch as you have done it (fed the hungry, clothed the naked, visited the imprisoned, sheltered the homeless), you have done it unto me." Admittedly the human need for demonstrable answers can be a compelling one and, it must be said, suggests that there is in the human psyche a kind of desire to be absolved from the exercise of freedom and a desire for finding relief in a world governed by predictability and determinism—the world which is the object of scientific investigation and the world in which no room is left for the exercise of free will because everything is determined by inexorable scientific law. "There is something servile in the habit of seeking after a law which we may obey. We may study the laws of matter at and for our convenience, but a successful life knows no law. It is an unfortunate discovery certainly, that of a law which binds us where we did not know before that we were bound. Live free, child of the mist,—and with respect to knowledge we are all children of the mist. The man who takes the liberty to live is superior to all laws, by virtue of his relation to the law-maker."[60] The God of the Christian faith wants believers who answer to an invitation to follow Christ and put into practice their devotion to Gospel values in a spirit of freedom. Those who characterize their religious faith with the language of certainty often alienate others and occasionally drive non-believers to derive pleasure from refuting fundamentalists' religious assertions and deflating their pompous self-assurance.

The conditions confronted by Neumann during his years serving the religious needs of relatively uneducated immigrants arguably did not demand a highly-developed apologetic. A "simple faith" defined Neumann's horizon. Neumann's nephew John Berger, in his biography of his uncle, underscores Neumann's feeling of discomfort in the company of the sophisticated and the well-to-do and his partiality for the uncultivated, whether humble factory workers such as those residents of Kensington or simple agrarian families that inhabited the rural exurbs of Philadelphia. As recounted by Berger, once, a day after having dined in the house of a wealthy, upper-class parishioner, Neumann was invited into the home of a poor, simple family: "What a difference between yesterday and today!," exclaimed Neuman. "Yesterday we were treated to a well-fed table, empty forms of politeness, and useless conversation; but today we were surrounded by the charming simplicity of a pious, Catholic home."[61] Within Neumann's rather circumscribed horizon there was little concern for an apologetic which would address the needs of the more prosperous descendants of those original immigrant families—descendants who would be gifted with access to a higher education. Without the authenticity of Neumann's "simple" faith being called into question or Neumann's partiality for less cultured believers being belittled, it may be asserted that the 20th century descendants of those humble immigrant families—that is, those beneficiaries of a higher education—would stand in need of a more highly-developed apologetic, one which places religious faith on a sound intellectual foundation. Thus there are consequences for undergoing a higher education; for those exposed to the learning accumulated over the past several centuries, a "simple" faith will not do. What Neumann did bequeath was an example of a spiritual life which liberated Neumann to devote his life serving others in imitation of Christ, in spite of the emotional limitations from which he suffered.

Neumann's Christian faith informed his behavior—his faith was not merely a matter of giving mental assent to a series of propositions with a religious theme.

When it comes to living in conformity with the Gospels, Neumann did not underestimate the obstacles within himself that might interfere with the task of living out the Christian message. That is to say, like many saints, he possessed an acute sense of his own sinfulness. Living in accord with Christ's commission, as contained in the Gospels, is a task, he knew, that required serious spiritual work. Therein lies the basis for the declaration of Neumann's sainthood, that he devoted his life to giving witness to God's love for all God's creatures. Such spiritual work included essentially the cultivation of theological virtues of faith, hope, and love. These are supernatural virtues, and, as such, sprout and bear fruit in soil not always initially well-prepared for that task. More than not being obstacles to his spiritual growth, Neumann's limitations can be seen as safeguarding him from vanity and arrogance.

Neumann's celebration of "simple faith" suggests that he was not beset with the kind of crises of faith not uncommon in the modern world. For Neumann, the obvious pastoral needs of the community of immigrants of his time had primacy of place—apologetics did not occupy first place among his priorities. As the claims of religious believers have come under greater scrutiny, however, apologetics can no longer remain on the back burner. Skepticism or simple indifference to religious commitment loom more prominently now, not so much, it seems, owing to doubts of a philosophical nature, but because of the ability of the good news of the Gospels to strain credibility by virtue of such news seeming to be too good to be true. Religious believers are often subject to being perceived as naïve. For that reason, on the part of the believer, simply professing faith without actualizing it in behavior renders it empty of meaning. The theological virtue of faith is strengthened through prayer as well as through action, and the strength thereby achieved brings with it the grace to weather inevitable episodes of doubt. Faith, like the other two theological virtues, is not always easy, especially in today's world. If the claims of Christianity, such as that of the resurrection of Jesus, were not incredible, there would be no need for the virtue of faith.

When it comes to the theological virtue of hope, Neumann's prayer life, particularly as evidenced in his journal, is seen to be imbued with his sense of trust in the promises of Christ. Neumann was not spared serious challenges to whatever sunny expectations that he may have had for a calm, conflict-free life. Hope sustained him during his dark days in Prague, during his four lonely years in western New York, and during his eight years as bishop when he had to cope with being somewhat of a disappointment to so many. Reasons for despair are never in short supply. "The mass of men lead lives of quiet desperation." That was Thoreau's assessment of his contemporaries. At the present moment the popularity of escape through substances that alter consciousness, either by delivering euphoria or engendering a state of oblivion, bears witness to the prevalence of despair. If "quiet desperation" is pervasive, so is desperation that is patently evident today—just take a stroll along Kensington Avenue in the vicinity of MacPherson Square. If the problems which beset the world did not at times inspire a sense of hopelessness, then there would be no need for the virtue of hope.

Neumann set a high standard for himself when it comes to the third theological virtue—the virtue of love, characterized by Paul as the "greatest" of the three theological virtues (1 Corinthians 13). Like faith and hope, love is not necessarily an easy virtue. It does not mean loving the loveable—it means loving everyone. The Gospels persistently present Christ as demonstrating a clear preference for society's outcastes and victims, such as lepers, tax collectors, beggars, prostitutes, those belonging to marginalized ethnic groups such as Samaritans, and to all those low on the social ladder. Neumann's ministry was conducted in service to immigrants, the beleaguered population targeted by the Nativists' ill will and who largely comprised those who prayed at Neumann's tomb at St. Peter's. If there was not a dispiriting level of injustice in the world begetting a multitude of society's victims, if there were no wars, no racism or sexism, if the world were free of walls and divisions and of the oppression of one population by another, the cogency of the theological virtue of love would be attenuated.

EPILOGUE

On several occasions over the past few years I have traveled to Kensington from my home in Delaware to take pictures for use in this narrative as well as to take stock of how Kensington has been transformed during the Post-Industrial Era. That there was an element of nostalgia in these excursions is readily acknowledged. That there is much to be lamented about what has become of Kensington is beyond question. Church and school closures, abandoned and boarded up warehouses, numerous shuttered storefronts, the disappearance of industrial landmarks owing to arson, are only a few features of the deterioration. Sweeping demographic change insured that no one remained with whom I might have had any history of mutual association. Of course there is nothing remarkable about change—change is something that can always be counted upon, at least in all material aspects of life.

If I may be permitted a final rumination, which will constitute the epilogue to this narrative, I would like to recount a recent visit to the neighborhood of the Shrine at St. Peter's. After spending some time one day at the Neumann Shrine gathering information at the Center's new museum, I set out with my camera in hand and walked along Girard Avenue in the direction of St. Michael's church. It was a crisp, late morning in November and the avenue was bathed in sunshine. As I took note of during my walk, a good amount of commercial activity remains in evidence along the busy thoroughfare, with numerous Latino eateries, nail salons, and small food markets. The Number 15 streetcar still plies the steel rails down the center of Girard Avenue—a throwback during a time when most of Philadelphia's streetcars have been supplanted by buses. Crossing 3rd Street with the intersection of 2nd Street just ahead, I contemplated the events of May, 1844. I imagined the Nativist mob reducing St. Michael's church to ashes and torching several blocks of rowhouses, then advancing across Girard Avenue (named Franklin Street until 1858) on their march south into the Northern Liberties with their sights on St. Augustine church.

Actualizing their dream of stifling the community in Kensington of newly-arrived immigrants, the Nativist mob scored only a short-lived triumph in the summer of 1844. The Nativist longing for a homogeneous citizenry, whether in terms of religion, ethnicity, or race, would endure and continue to confront the nation with the questions: *On what is the American identity founded? Is it founded upon race, religion, ethnicity, or is it founded upon a shared commitment to civic ideals, such as liberty, equality, and justice for all?* These reflections were abruptly disrupted when I was stopped short at 2nd Street by the sight of a newly-installed piece of street sculpture.

On a small triangular plaza formed where American Street and 2nd Street meet at Girard Avenue, stands a statue of Don Quixote mounted on his horse, Rocinante. The statue would not warrant a second look if it were positioned along the Benjamin Franklin Parkway or on East River Drive in Fairmount Park, but here in Kensington one does not expect to see a piece of public art on display, excepting perhaps a brightly-painted mural on the side of a building. It so happens that the Quixote sculpture was a gift from a city in Spain—the city of Ciudad Real in the region of La Mancha, and was presented for installation in 1997 at the edge of the American Street Empowerment Zone. The program of designating empowerment zones identifies neighborhoods which have suffered economic decline during the Post-Industrial Era and provides grants for economic development and beautification. Both Upper and Lower Kensington have a substantial Latino population and it may be presumed that Quixote, as the central figure of the canon of literary works written in Spanish, is appropriately placed where the Spanish language is often heard. Facing south with lance held aloft and mounted on Rocinante, Quixote has witnessed the demolition of the old Schmidt's brewery complex and the construction of the "Piazza at Schmidt's," a mixed commercial and residential complex presumably earmarked for well-heeled young professionals. Behind the knight errant, where once significant urban deterioration was evident, is a scene of robust activity. The air bristles with the noise of construction projects—the incessant din of hammering and the drone of heavy equipment. All this can only mean that the "G" word can be applied to Lower Kensington. The gentrification that has been transforming neighboring Northern Liberties and Fishtown is spilling over into Lower Kensington.

Standing by the Quixote sculpture at 2nd and Girard, I could see the tall spire of St. Michael's church several blocks to the north on 2nd Street. Over the past several decades the church has served communities of immigrants, largely from Latino countries, just as the church had served communities of beleaguered Irish immigrants of poor means in the 19th century. Kensington has maintained its identity as a haven for immigrants for well over a century. But the recently-installed Quixote statue and the construction activity abounding in the vicinity indicate that Lower Kensington is on the radar of developers. There is irony implicated in the prospect of the streets of Lower Kensington becoming endowed with the ambiance of trendiness. This was once a neighborhood of hoagie shops and of corner taprooms emitting the stench of stale beer, of the carts of soft pretzel vendors, and of groups of street toughs establishing proprietorship over their favored street corner. This neighborhood that was the site of the sanguinary and destructive Nativist riots, has now been acquiring chic restaurants and cafes, craft beer pubs, and high-end apartment complexes. No doubt the signature residence of Kensington—the red brick rowhouse which served as the modestly-priced residence for generations of the families of blue-collar workers—will be rechristened the "townhouse," as such humble abodes are spruced up and stamped with a hefty price tag. A profound neighborhood population shift is likely in store. The close-knit communities of the 19th century German and Irish immigrants and their 20th century descendants, as well as those of the Latino arrivals in the 20th century, will likely give way to more affluent inhabitants. The bishop who felt at home among simple and uncultivated immigrants will find himself surrounded by the trappings of urban chic.

    As I continued on my way north along 2nd Street, I remained preoccupied by the Cervantean hero encountered unexpectedly on Girard Avenue. The figure of Quixote, while admittedly fictional, conjures up thoughts about the nature of heroism, just as the Neumann Shrine several blocks west elicits reflection about the heroism of sainthood. Both Neumann and Quixote are avatars of unwavering commitment, and both endured derision for their manner of living out their commitments. Quixote came to his commitment late. He was in midlife when he found himself disenchanted with the world he witnessed around him with what he saw as the drabness brought about by the growing spirit of mercantilism, materialism, and shabby commercialism. The times had become drained of any transforming passion. His recourse was to devote himself to devouring novels of the age of chivalry which seemed to be an time full of passion and vigorous idealism. The vitality of this age, however, was well-nigh spent by Quixote's lifetime. Upon becoming satiated with tales of Medieval chivalry, and as testimony to the power of reading, he became mentally unhinged, equipping himself with the accoutrements of Medieval knighthood. With armor, lance, and steed, he embarked upon a career of knight errancy, his advanced age notwithstanding. His determination to do battle with agents of evil was not to be deterred, even by reality. The unending entertainment value of the novel derives from Quixote's sacrifice of sound reality-testing, a sacrifice made all the more comic because of the knight's adoption of all the austere self-denial which Medieval knighthood demanded. While he could count upon being humored by those who knew him, he suffered frequent beatings by those who had no patience with him when he attacked those whom he inaccurately perceived as malevolent during his valiant quest.

 As I approached Saint Michael's, I interrupted my ruminations about Don Quixote to take note that there is little bustle today in the vicinity of the church. It is certainly nothing like it must have been when the Nanny Goat Market and the Cohocksink Railroad Station generated a brisk street life in the 1840s. What animation exists currently is largely accounted for by those engaged in residential construction projects.

Having completed my photographic objectives at Saint Michael's, I decided to head north on foot in the direction of Upper Kensington. The tranquility along Front Street, consequent to the diminution of commercial activity along the once busy thoroughfare, was broken only by the clatter of the occasional passing of the el train overhead. Prominent along the street now is the Kensington High School for the Creative and Performing Arts. Recessed away from the el, the sleek and airy building with its bright metal siding is girded with much green space, something not traditionally seen in Kensington. More greenery comes into view when approaching the neatly-mown athletic field of the Shissler Recreation Center astride the high school. Kensington, at least Lower Kensington, is gradually becoming more arrayed in green.

As I turned onto Kensington Avenue upon reaching York Street, the ominous feeling induced by this stretch of the avenue began to surface, as in times past. The shuttered storefronts and empty shops interrupted by the occasional parcel of vacant space serving as a niche for rusting cars or other abandoned debris reveal a world in the grip of neglect. But coming into view was an animated assemblage on the sidewalk, disclosing a center of unexpected human activity. It was the Franciscan Inn, an unassuming storefront where clothing, food, and hospitality for the indigent can be obtained. The Franciscan charism is alive and well in Kensington.

Continuing north along the avenue, I noted additional agencies devoted to providing for the needs of migrant communities, the homeless, and those suffering from addictions. At the corner of Lehigh and Kensington Avenues at the former site of the Starlight Ballroom next to the Visitation Church, is the Community Center at Visitation which is operated by the Archdiocese of Philadelphia. Further north, several blocks west of K&A on Allegheny Avenue, is the Welcome Center which is staffed by the Sisters of St. Joseph. Undaunted by the closure of the Ascension, where the order has discharged their commission to educate children through much of the 20th century, the sisters have embraced a new charism—to meet the needs of migrant communities.

Amid all the contemporary flag-waving hyper-patriotism and disingenuous lip-service paid the Christian values, which generally serve as camouflage for racism and Nativist bigotry, there are those who have been summoned by the precepts of the Gospels to serve the neglected communities bearing the brunt of post-industrial urban deterioration. Anyone with an aversion to religious hypocrisy will find no grist for their anti-religious rancor at centers such as the Franciscan Inn or the Welcome Center staffed by the Sisters of Saint Joseph. What is on view is a Gospel-driven commitment to serve others, carried out without any quixotic need to distort reality, or to divorce professed beliefs from action.

I ended this long day of walking by boarding the el at the Allegheny Station in order to head back to Girard Avenue. However much of the face of Kensington has been transformed during the Post-Industrial era, the el has continued to course through the length of the gritty district for a century. Not everything changes.

APPENDIX A

TIMELINE

1717   Fairhill mansion is constructed by wealthy entrepreneur and Quaker Isaac Norris

1798   Rebellion of 1798 in Ireland, waged by the United Irishmen, largely consisting of Scotch-Irish Presbyterians and bent upon ridding Ireland of British control; The rebellion failed, leading to substantial emigration of Scotch-Irish to America, many being by trade who found their way to Kensington.

1811   John Neumann, 4th bishop of Philadelphia, born in Prachatitz, Bohemia

1820   District of Kensington is incorporated in March

1820s   Substantial immigration of Irish Catholics into America begins

1830-1831   Cholera epidemic breaks out in Philadelphia

1833   Cornerstone of St. Michael's church laid by Bishop Kenrich at 2nd and Masters Streets

1834   The Kensington Rail Depot opens at Front and Berks Streets

1835   Hughes-Breckinridge debates take place in Philadelphia

1836   John Neumann arrives in the United States

1840-1842   "Railroad Riots" take place in Kensington; residents of Kensington obstruct attempt of the Philadelphia and Trenton Railroad Company to lay rails in Front Street

1842   John Neumann is professed as a Redemptorist

1842   Francis Kenrich, bishop of Philadelphia, sends a letter to the Philadelphia Board of Education on November 10 requesting that Catholic school children be excused from Bible-reading class, or be allowed to read the Douay-Rheims version—the approved Catholic version

1843   Saint Peter's Catholic Church built on Girard Avenue at 5th Street in Kensington

1844   Nativist George Shifler shot and killed in Kensington by shots allegedly fired from the Hibernia Hose Company during a Nativist rally

1844   Nativist Riots take place, May 7-8; St Michael's church and several blocks of rowhouses are torched; dozens killed

1845   Potato crop in Ireland fails, afflicted by blight; famine lasts four years

1846   Cornerstone is laid for new Saint Michael's church

1847   John Neumann is named Superior-General of Redemptorist in the United States

1848   John Neumann becomes a naturalized American citizen

1852   John Neumann is named bishop of Philadelphia

1852   Episcopal Hospital on Lehigh Avenue opens

1853   Papal Nuncio Gaetano Bedini makes official visit to the

United States, arriving in New York on June 30th. He remains in the U.S. for six months, and offers an assessment of the condition of the diocese of Philadelphia and of Neumann's fitness for his post as bishop

1853   Saint Michael's Elementary School opens in Kensington at 2nd and Masters Streets

1854   Consolidation of Kensington into city of Philadelphia

1854   Robert T. Conrad is elected mayor of Philadelphia, candidate of the Whig and American (Know-Nothing) parties.

1856   The Picnic Train tragedy, July 17th; more than sixty deaths, most of them being students of St Michael's religious education program, as two trains of the North Pennsylvania Railroad collide head-on.

1857   John Neumann's nephew, John Berger, arrives in the United States from Bohemia

1860   Bishop John Neumann dies on July 5th; interred at St. Peter's church Kensington; James Wood becomes Philadelphia's fifth bishop

1869   Knights of Labor founded by Uriah Stephens at a meeting in a rowhouse on the 2300 block of E. Coral Street, Kensington.

1872   Saint Boniface Church on Diamond Street is dedicated

1877   Visitation Church on Lehigh Avenue is dedicated

1880   Lucretia Mott dies and is interred in Quaker Burial G round in Fairhill

1884   Biography of John Neumann by John Berger is published

1887   Kensington Hospital for Women opens on Diamond Street in Kensington

1898   McPherson Square Library opens in the Webster Mansion in McPherson Square

1890   Northeast Manual Training School opens in Kensington on Girard Avenue at Howard Street

1899   Ascension Catholic Church on Westmoreland St is dedicated

1900   Ascension Elementary School opens

1903   "March of the Mill Children" launched on July 7th; led by Mother Jones, it departs from Labor Lyceum at 2nd and Cambria Streets.

1905   New school building for the Northeast Manual Training School opens on Lehigh Avenue between 7th & 8th Streets.

1911   Northeast Manual Training School renamed Northeast Public High School

1914   Seaman Charles Allen Smith killed at Vera Cruz, Mexico, on April 22nd, during a military operation; memorial service held at McPherson Square on May 13th; tens of thousands attend to pay respects to the Kensington native

1915   New McPherson Square Library building is dedicated

1917   Charles Allen Smith Memorial dedicated in McPherson Square

1919   St. Boniface Commercial School for girls opens

1921   John Neumann is declared "Venerable," first step in process toward sainthood.

1922   Frankford el is completed and dedicated on Nov 4

1923   Babe Ruth makes appearance in charity semi-pro game at Boger Field, "I" & Tioga Sts.

1926   Northeast Catholic High School opens on Torresdale Ave.

1930   Textile workers at Aberle Mill at "C" and Clearfield Sts. go on strike; union member and striker Carl Mackley is shot and killed by strikebreaker on March 6th; memorial service for Mackley on March 9th held at McPherson draws more than 30,000

1933   Protest march held in Kensington by opponents of "Open Sundays" law; rally by protesters at McPherson Square draws more than 6,000

1934   William Casey named pastor of the Ascension

1945   Kensington Hospital for Women closes; opens the following year as Kensington General Hospital

1952   Biography of John Neumann by Michael Curley is published

1960   Racist mob trashes rowhouse at 3115 "C" St in Kensington on September30th to prevent occupancy of the house by African-American family

1961   Frankford el derailment at York-Dauphin el station on Dec 26th. One is killed; dozens are injured

1967   William Casey, pastor emeritus of Ascension, dies

1977   John Neumann is canonized, first male American saint

1979   John Bromley & Sons textile mill at "B" St and Lehigh Avenue destroyed by fire

1979   St. Francis Inn opens at 2441 Kensington Avenue

1994   Novel *3rd and Indiana* by Steve Lopez is published

1994   Quaker Lace Company factory complex at 4th St and Lehigh Avenue reduced to ashes in September

2003   Archdiocese of Philadelphia opens the Cardinal Bevilacqua Community Center at 2646 Kensington Avenue. Management of the center is transferred to the Visitation BVM parish in 2010, and the center becomes the Community Center at Visitation.

2003   Sisters of St. Joseph Welcome Center opens at 728 E. Allegheny Avenue

2006   St. Boniface Church closes

2009   The Sankofa Freedom Academy Charter School, built on the Freedom School model, opens at 2501 Kensington Avenue, offering grades K-12.

2010   Northeast Catholic High School closes

2011   The building once occupied by the Thomas A. Edison High school at 7th and Lehigh is destroyed by fire

2011   The Kensington High School for the Creative and Performing Arts opens at 1901 N. Front Street

2012   St. Boniface church is demolished

2012   The Archdiocese of Philadelphia announces in September the closure of the Ascension parish

APPENDIX B

WORKS CITED

Berger, John. Life of Right Rev. John N. Neumann, D.D., of the Congregation of the Most Holy Redeemer, 4th Bishop of Philadelphia. Benziger Bros., N.Y. 1884.

Billington, Ray Allen. The Protestant Crusade, 1800-1860: A Study of the Origins of American Nativism. MacMillan, New York. 1938.

Curley, Michael. Bishop John Neumann, C.SS.R., Fourth Bishop of Philadelphia. Bishop Neumann Center, Philadelphia, PA. 1952

Chadwick, Owen. "Eucharist and Christology in the Nestorian Controversy." The Journal of Theological Studies, v.2, n.2, pgs. 145-164.

Hughes, John and Breckinridge, John. *A Discussion of the Question, Is the Roman Catholic Religion, in Any or in All its Principles or Doctrines, Inimical to Civil or Religious Liberty? And of the Question, Is the Presbyterian Religion, in Any or in All its Principles or Doctrines, Inimical to Civil or Religious Liberty?* W. Dickson, 1855.

James, William. *The Varieties of Religious Experience.* Library of America, New York, 1987.

Milano, Kenneth W. The Philadelphia Nativist Riots. The History Press, Charleston, SC. 2013.

Neumann, John N. *The Autobiography of St. John Neumann, C.SS.R.* Daughters of St. Paul, Boston, 1977.

Newman, John Henry. "Curiosity a Temptation to Sin," contained in *Selected Sermons*, Prayers, and Devotions, Vintage Books, New York, 1999. Pgs. 305-312.

Penn, William. Some Fruits of Solitude in Reflections and Maxims. (*originally published in London in 1693*). Applewood Books, Bedford, MA. 1996.

Rush, Alfred C. "The Permission to Bury John Neumann in St. Peter's, Philadelphia," http://www.santalfonsoedintorni.it/Spicilegium/24/SH-24-1976(II)476-484.pdf

Schell, Jonathan. The Fate of the Earth. Library of America, New York. 2020.

Shaw, Richard. D*agger John: the unquiet life and times of Archbishop John Hughes of* New York. Paulist Press, 1977.

Thoreau, Henry David. "Walking." Collected Essays and Poems. Literary Classics of the United States, Library of America, New York, 2001.

Weigley, Russell F. "The Border City in the Civil War: 1854-1865," in *Philadelphia: A 300-Year History*, ed. By Russell F. Weigley. W. W. Norton & Company, New York, 1982.

Wood, James Frederic. "Some Early Letters of James F. Wood from Rome, Cincinnati, and Philadelphia." Records of the American Catholic Historical Society of Philadelphia., vol. 83, no. 1, March 1972. pgs. 37-61.

Yacovazzi, Cassandra L. Escaped Nuns: True Womanhood and the Campaign against Convents in Antebellum America. Oxford University Press, New York. 2018.

"The Full Particulars of the Late Riots, with a View of the Burning of the Catholic Churches, St. Michaels & St. Augustines." (Philadelphia, 1844) Catholica Collection. Digital Library @ Villanova University.

FOOTNOTES

1 Vonorthphilly.org
2 *Philadelphia Inquirer.* "Ruth scores only run for Ascension," Sep 5, 1923.
3 Ralph Waldo Emerson. *Nature,* Library of America, New York, 1983, p.7*Philadelphia Tribune.* "Little Children Carried Hate Signs in Kensington Mob," October 1st, 1960.
4 *Philadelphia Tribune.* "Little Children Carried Hate Signs in Kensington Mob," October 1st, 1960.
5 *www.facebook.com/PhiladelphiaStoriesby Bob McNulty*
6 *Philadelphia Public Ledger.* "35,000 at funeral for strike victim," March 10th, 1930.
7 *Philadelphia Inquirer.* "Throngs protest open Sunday plan," *October 22nd, 1933.*
8 *Philadelphia Inquirer.* "Fire hits old mill in Kensington," July 30th, 1979.
9 *Philadelphia Inquirer.* "Fire destroys warehouse and 12 nearby homes," *September 20th, 1994.*
10 *www.phillychurchproject.com*
11 11*www.phillydesegregation.weebly.com/study-of-northeast-high-schools-move-In-1957*
12 *Richard Sand.* Edison 64: a Tragedy in Vietnam and at Home. *Righter's Mill Press, Princeton, 2019.*
13 Edison 64 – Names and Faces – facebook.com
14 *Philadelphia Inquirer.* "El jumps track, one dead, 35 hurt," December 27th, 1961.
15 William Penn. Some Fruits of Solitude. Harvard Classics, 1909. P.62
16 Kenneth Milano. The Philadelphia Nativist Riots. pgs. 41-43.
17 http://inthepastlane.com/nativism-yesterday-and-today/
18 I am grateful to Brian Daley, S.J. of Notre Dame University for directing my attention to the article, "Eucharist and Christology in the Nestorian Controversy," by Owen Chadwick, found in The Journal of Theological Studies, Volume II, Issue 2, October 1951,

pgs. 145-164. Chadwick highlights the assertion of Cyril: " . . . the flesh of the Lord is life-giving and the particular property of the Logos himself who is from God the Father.")

[19] *Richard Shaw*. Dagger John: the Unquiet Life and Times of Archbishop *John Hughes of New York, p.82.*

[20] *Hughes, John, and John Breckinridge. A Discussion of the Question, Is the Roman Catholic Religion, in Any or in All Its Principles or Doctrines, Inimical to Civil or Religious Liberty? And of the Question, Is the Presbyterian Religion, in Any or in All Its Principles or Doctrines, Inimical to Civil or Religious Liberty? W. Dickson, 1855.*

[21] bid, p.20.

[22] Ibid, p.60.

[23] Ibid, p.199.

[24] Ibid, p.348.

[25] Ibid, p.350.

[26] *The incident is recounted in a publication of the Philadelphia Keighton Printing House, 1891, entitled Kensington: a city within a city, on pages xiv-xv. No author is listed for the publication.*

[27] p. 4 "The Full Particulars of the Late Riots, with a View of the Burning of the Catholic Churches, St. Michael's and St. Augustine" is available online https://babel.hathitrust.org/cgi/pt?id=uc1.31175035253064&view=1up&seq=16

[28] Phillychurchproject.com

[29] *Russell F. Weigley. "The Border City in Civil War: 1854-1865," from Philadelphia: A 300-year History. p.368.*

[30] Ibid. p.370.

[31] *"The Restriction of Immigration," speech delivered by Henry Cabot Lodge In the Senate, March 16, 1896* https://www.nationalists.org/library/america/henry-lodge-speech-1896.html

[32] www.findagrave.com/cemetery/2193353/saintmichaels-cemetery

[33] "Appalling Calamity: Collision on the North Pennsylvania Railroad," New York Times, July 18, 1856.

[34] lasalleacademy.net

[35] liguorian.org

[36] *As quoted by Michael J. Curley, in* Bishop John Neumann, C.SS.R.: A Biography. Bishop Neumann Center, Phila., 1952. P.284.

[37] John Berger. The Life of Right Rev. John N. Neumann, D.D., Benziger Brothers, New York, 1884.

[38] Berger, p.196.

[39] Ibid. p.179.

[40] Ibid. p.179.

[41] Ibid. p.428.
[42] Ibid. p.216.
[43] *As quoted in Curley, p.151.*
[44] As quoted in Curley, p.145.
[45] Berger, p. 7.
[46] *Ibid. pgs.420-430.*
[47] *Ibid. p.426.*
[48] *As quoted in Curley, p.281.*
[49] *As quoted in Curley, p.331.*
[50] *From letter of James Wood to Alessandro Cardinal Barnabo, Sep 15, 1858, in "Some Early Letters of James F. Wood," in* Records of the American Catholic Historical Society, *vol.83, March 1972, no.1, p.53.*
[51] *Alfred C. Rush,* "The Permission to bury Saint John Neumann in Saint Peter's," http://www.santalfonsoedintorni.it/Spicilegium/24/SH-24-1976(II)476-484.pdf
[52] *John N. Neumann,* The Autobiography of St. John Neumann, *C.SS.R., Daughters of St. Paul, Boston, 1977.*
[53] *John Nepomucene Neumann's Spiritual Journal* file:///home/chronos/u-efaaafc3caacb2cd9dcc93fafed4cb873e02337a/MyFiles/Downloads/SH-26-1978(I)009-074.pdf *The Journal is also available at: The Catholic Historical Research Center of the Archdiocese of Philadelphia at 6740 Roosevelt Blvd., 19149*
[54] John Neumann, p.28.
[55] *William James. The Varieties of Religious Experience. p.121*
[56] John Henry Newman. "Curiosity a Temptation to Sin," found in *Selected Sermons, Prayers, and Devotions* by John Henry Newman, Vintage Books, New York, 1999. P.305.
[57] Curley, p. 362.
[58] *Thomas Merton,* Life and Holiness, *Image Books, Doubleday, New York. 1963. P. 75.*
[59] *Jonathan Schell.* The Fate of the Earth. *Library of America, New York, 2020. P. 98*
[60] Henry David Thoreau. "Walking." Collected Essays and Poems, Library of America, New York, 2001. P. 250.
[61] Berger, p. 424.

Made in the USA
Middletown, DE
02 November 2024